SLLA Crash Course

SLLA Crash Course

Approaches for Success

Wafa Hozien

ROWMAN & LITTLEFIELD
Lanham • Boulder • New York • London

Published by Rowman & Littlefield
A wholly owned subsidiary of The Rowman & Littlefield Publishing Group, Inc.
4501 Forbes Boulevard, Suite 200, Lanham, Maryland 20706
www.rowman.com

Unit A, Whitacre Mews, 26–34 Stannary Street, London SE11 4AB

British Library Cataloguing in Publication Information Available

Library of Congress Cataloging-in-Publication Data Available
ISBN 978-1-4758-2784-2 (cloth : alk.paper)
ISBN 978-1-4758-2785-9 (pbk. : alk. paper)
ISBN 978-1-4758-2786-6 (electronic)

∞™ The paper used in this publication meets the minimum requirements of American National
Standard for Information Sciences—Permanence of Paper for Printed Library Materials, ANSI/
NISO Z39.48-1992.

Printed in the United States of America

For Isra, for always being there, for always making me smile,
and making this happen;

For my mother and father, for the strength they give me; and

For my children, for your understanding.

Thank you all for your support through all these years.

Contents

Foreword

SLLA Crash Course: *Approaches for Success* is a wonderful resource for those preparing to take the School Leaders Licensure Assessment (SLLA) or those assisting the preparation of others to take the SLLA. This comprehensive reader-friendly guide provides users with a wealth of information, strategies, and useful tips that will increase one's readiness to successfully complete the SLLA.

There is a significant difference between preparation and readiness. Preparing for the SLLA does not guarantee your readiness to successfully complete the exam. College and university programs across the country enroll and graduate candidates from their principal licensure programs prepared but not ready for the SLLA or success as a school leader.

During my tenure at the National Association of Secondary School Principals (NASSP), I was privileged to deliver many presentations to groups of principals. I frequently asked them this question, "How did you get to be as good as you are?" Their responses always followed the same pattern, regardless of the state or region of the country: learning on the job, willingness to take risks, mentors, trial and error, and feedback. Seldom did a person respond that their preparation program was a factor in their current success. To add perspective to these thoughts, I often ask my physician, dentist, and accountant how their preparation program impacts their daily practice, and their responses clearly state that their preparation is instrumental in their current practice. This is an unfortunate reality for those preparing for the SLLA without the benefit of practical experience as a school leader.

I had the pleasure of participating in the development of the original *Interstate School Leaders Licensure Consortium (ISLLC) Standards* in the late 90s, cochaired the development of the *Educational Leadership Policy Standards (ISLLC 2008)*, and chaired the Educational Leadership Constituent Council (ELCC) for ten years. Professional standards' development and application contributes to making better principals, a precursor to making principals better. I saw the impact that the *ELCC Standards*, the program version of the *Professional Standards for School Leaders*, had on increasing the quality of principal preparation programs. The latest version of the standards, *Professional Standards for Educational Leaders (2015)*, reflects the continuing evolution for the profession. Each new iteration of the standards clearly echoes the changes in the "art of the practice" and increases the expectations for the profession and the stakes for those planning to enter the field of school leadership.

High-stakes testing is a tool that the policy community uses to ensure competence by practitioners. The SLLA is a high-stakes test that serves as a barrier to entrance in the profession. While specific details of administration and scoring vary from state to state, the SLLA is typically taken prior to any significant practical experience.

What are the success factors that can increase your readiness to successfully complete the SLLA? Quality preparation certainly increases the opportunities for success. *SLLA Crash Course*: *Approaches for Success* is a quality preparation tool. I am impressed by the content. From the focus on the *Professional Standards for Educational Leaders (2015)*, to the structure of the SLLA exam and how the exam is scored, the author provides useful information on approaching multiple choice responses, constructed-response questions, effective use of time, and approaches and tips. Practice tests are included in addition to a constructed-response practice tool. This book should be required reading for anyone preparing for the SLLA.

Research clearly indicates that principal quality is a major factor in school quality. In an ever-increasingly complex world, school principals have to adapt to the changes that confront every community and school. The quest to "make better principals" begins with a quality preparation program, a rigorous clinical experience, and successful completion of the SLLA. *SLLA Crash Course*: *Approaches for Success* serves to minimize the lack of experience in preparing for the SLLA. We know that experience is the best teacher, but absent experience, let this book be your best teacher and coach in ensuring your successful completion of the SLLA and opening the gateway for your entrance into the profession.

Richard A. Flanary
President, Flanary Educational Consulting,
and former Deputy Executive Director for Programs & Services,
the National Association of Secondary School Principals (NASSP)

Introduction

If you have this book in your hand, you are, most likely, looking to take the School Leaders Licensure Assessment (SLLA). That, potentially, means you are an aspiring school leader. There are some important components to being a school leader outlined by a group of school officials called the Council of Chief State School Officers (CCSSO). These components or Interstate School Leaders Licensure Consortium (ISLLC) Standards that this exam is based on are explained throughout this book for you to understand and help you achieve your goals.

It is helpful to understand the overarching themes on which the SLLA is built before we get into the details of the standards. As introduced in the upcoming sections, the ten standards are based upon school administrative practices. So you have to think like a school principal, even though you might not be one yet. Put on your thinking cap and imagine you now have the responsibilities of a school leader. First and foremost you are concerned with the curricula and instructional leadership, then school community leadership, and administrative leadership. Before we get into the specifics that are covered on the SLLA, let us take a step back and understand the exam and what is involved in passing this assessment.

The SLLA is a licensure examination developed by the Educational Testing Service (ETS), with the ISLLC. This study book is designed to assist you in preparing to take this test by providing you with both general and specific information regarding test-taking and the SLLA itself.

What Is SLLA?

School leaders are entrusted with overseeing the education of students. Because their work is so important, the public demands that they be held to the highest professional and ethical standards. Legislation and licensing boards in many states have responded by establishing licensing programs to evaluate each potential principal's relevant knowledge, skills, and abilities.

The SLLA was developed to provide a thorough, fair, and carefully validated assessment for states to use as part of the licensure process for school leaders. It reflects the most current research and the professional judgment and experience of educators across the country, and is based on both a national job analysis study and a set of standards for school leaders identified by the ISLLC.

ETS constructs and administers the SLLA exams for the College Board, which is a nonprofit agency whose goal is to increase access to higher education. The College Board is known for programs like the SAT, AP, and CLEP tests. Six thousand educational institutions participate in the College Board programs.

If you are in education, you've heard about the SLLA exam for school principal certification, even if you are in one of the states that do not require this test for certification. School leadership is both an art and a science. What this book will do is to help you on your path to becoming a school leader and gaining certification. The SLLA test is the licensure exam for aspiring school leaders and educators in these different states requiring this exam.

In general, educational leadership academic support programs are not uniform across the country. The most basic programs provide voluntary workshops in passing the leadership assessment, writing skills, or analysis. More elaborate programs might pretest incoming students to place them in remedial programs at the beginning of their study and follow the student through the entire two-year program with a series of workshops, classes, and tests both voluntary and mandatory. Once students are admitted and matriculate, it becomes the school's responsibility to provide an academic support program to aid the student in successfully completing school and SLLA passage. Most online universities, or smaller colleges and universities, do not provide such support. This is where this book comes in. It is meant as a guide to get the student through the SLLA.

Unlike other majors, which usually require a specific background, there is no particular major required for educational leadership school admission. Applicants rely on a number of sources to choose education schools that they wish to apply to, including word-of-mouth, college of education fairs, and U.S. New and World Report rankings. These sources may not be accurate in their assessment of educational leadership school qualities that the applicant thinks may be important in their selection. This may be a particular problem for first-generation college or graduate students who might not understand the criteria used to select an educational leadership or administration school.

Becoming a school leader is more of an art than a science; beyond the SLLA, professionals use a combination of the following factors to determine suitability for an applicant's admission to school leadership positions: prior graduate work, work experience, extracurricular activities, volunteer experience, and other unique experiences the applicant may share during the application process. Each school has its own scoring system to determine suitability, including the following: post-baccalaureate education, work experience, personal experience, and other factors created by the school district or education professionals.

The applicant chooses what additional information to provide the school selection committee without the benefit of guidance as to what selection committees are really looking for in making the determination. School selection committees use a variety of systems to evaluate potential school leadership candidates, which include but are not limited to assigning points to the various factors, check-off lists, and committee member advocates. On occasion, the decision may come down to the writing sample from the cover letter; anecdotally, school principals have revealed they put little effort into the cover letter since they knew it was their resume that was most important and they did not think it could be the difference between acceptance and denial of their application for a school leadership position.

In some states, potential administrators may gain certification by successfully passing the SLLA. This book attempts to be an aid to passing the SLLA so as to ease the route to administrative licensure in an effective way, thereby placing quality candidates into entry-level assistant principal positions by providing the preparation for entry-level administrators. This book is meant to help the student receive certification through passing this examination.

The preparation of examination takers is important to achieving a passing score on the SLLA. Surveys revealed that both principals and assistant principals believed that much of what administrators needed to know is learned on the job. Interviews revealed three key findings. First, that states should continue to hire administrators through the examination route. Second, professional development for assistant principals should be focused on relevant skills such as communication, problem-solving, and time management. Finally, school districts and universities should look at creating new partnerships that aim at building the capacity of administrators once they are on the job.

School principal shortages have been an ongoing dilemma that states have confronted for the past three decades. Many states have responded to this shortage of qualified principal applicants by creating alternative routes to administrative licensure. In many states, an administrative aspirant can gain licensure through two primary paths: a traditional university program or a state-approved program that is usually a collaboration between a local district and an institution of higher education. In some states, however, there is a third option: passing the SLLA.

The SLLA is a four examination created by the ETS that accounts for leadership quality and consistency, and is based upon the ten ISLLC Standards (Bryant, Hessel, & Isernhagen, 2002). Although this route seems to be quick and easy, there are problems associated with it. Today, some school districts and universities are creating new partnerships that aim at building the capacity of administrators once they are on the job.

This book is divided into three parts: understanding the SLLA exam and all that it encompasses, proven study strategies to help you to successfully pass the SLLA, and finally, practice tests containing two multiple choice sections and an essay question section that are similar to the ones on the exam. Take these practice tests often so as to familiarize yourself with the question format and the language of the SLLA.

Part I

EXAM FORMAT AND SPECIFICS

Section 1

The Structure of the Exam

The School Leaders Licensure Assessment (SLLA) exam is separated into two sections: multiple choice and essay questions called constructed-response questions. All answers will be based on what experience new education leaders should've learned from graduate-level work with education leadership and administration courses or professional experiences while working in the school system. Test takers have four hours to complete the entire test. Calculators are not allowed for either section.

TEST FORMAT

Section I—100 multiple choice questions, 140 minutes, worth 70 percent of the test
Section II—seven shorter constructed-response types of questions in which you have only 10–12 minutes to answer each, 100 minutes, worth 30 percent of the test

SCORING THE TEST QUESTIONS

Of the six sections that will be used for the test, the results will be divided into eight sections separating 100 multiple choice questions from seven constructed-response questions.

The six sections within the SLLA test will be grouped into the following:

Vision and Goals: The focus area is shared commitments for implementing, teaching, and techniques for improvement of these visions and goals.

Teaching and Learning: The focus area looks at the technical end of teaching, such as assessments, accountability, curriculum, instruction, and ways of creating and maintaining a professional culture.

Organizational Systems and Safety: The focus area also examines the technical side of an educational background through operation systems, fiscal and human resources, and the welfare and safety of all students and staff.

Collaboration with Key Stakeholders: The focus area is the cultural environment of an educational facility, including working with family members and the community, listening and working on stakeholder interests and needs, and utilizing community resources to implement shared educational interests.

Education System: The focus area is incorporating local decisions into bigger educational policies.

Ethics and Integrity: The focus is on acting with integrity and in accordance with professional norms to promote student success. Modelling personal and professional ethics, integrity, justice and fairness, and expects the same of others.

There is substantial intersection in the integration of the individual competencies because a school principal does not do his/her job in sections nor is the principalship a compartmentalized job. Hourly roles and tasks are interconnected. While putting out the storms of an average school day, does the typical principal say, "Wait," and is this Standard 1 Vision of the School or Standard 4 the Curriculum? Absolutely not. This is why you should know the standards inside and out and internalize their components so that you can respond reflectively and instinctively. Before getting into the detailed analysis of the standards within the next sections of this book, let us discuss specific components about the SLLA format and the actual Interstate School Leaders Licensure Consortium (ISLLC) standards.

Professional Standards for Education Leaders in 2015

These are standards approved by the National Policy Board for Education Administration geared toward all educational stakeholders. Questions may focus on the following:

Standard 1. Mission, Vision, and Core Values
Standard 2. Ethics and Professional Norms
Standard 3. Equity and Cultural Responsiveness
Standard 4. Curriculum, Instruction, and Assessment
Standard 5. Community of Care and Support for Students
Standard 6. Professional Capacity of School Personnel
Standard 7. Professional Community for Teachers and Staff
Standard 8. Meaningful Engagement of Families and Community
Standard 9. Operations and Management
Standard 10. School Improvement

KEY IDEAS TO KEEP IN MIND FOR THE SLLA EXAM

While preparing for the SLLA exam, here are key ideas to understand before completing the exam.

- Understand Standards-based instructional programs
- Increase rigorous curriculum activities
- Collaborate and maintain teamwork with teachers and other staff members to monitor student work and progress throughout any required timeframe

- Standards-based instructional programs
- Rigorous curriculum activities
- Teamwork with teachers and other staff members to monitor student work and progress throughout any required timeframe
- Make sure students are meeting the school's guidelines for instructional programs
- Assist in guiding faculty members through rigorous testing and instruction projects
- Monitor professional development for faculty members
- Analyze student curriculum and instruction to meet program evaluation methods
- Be equipped to handle diverse, personalized needs for each student's learning habits
- Provide an environment where students are given the opportunity to be challenged and enjoy a safe, effective educational environment
- Utilize teaching activities to help students be able to get over educational opportunities and career achievements for the future
- Encourage an open-door policy for faculty to be able to share concerns with educational leaders
- Meet with staff to give constructive, honest feedback to help better assist them in an educational environment

Most of the answers on the test will revolve around the key points above and will require the test taker to create or properly identify the resolution to potential problems within the schooling system. Textbooks, state-standard publications, and sample tests are encouraged in order to get a grasp of the type of content that will be used in the final exam.

FOCUS QUESTIONS: LEARNING THE CONCEPTS

While most of the questions will require knowing a combination of policies, teaching habits and state-standard skills, study questions with the standard after them are intended for memorization of an amalgam of concepts. As provided for the reader in the Exam section at the end of this book, so as the reader will understand which standard s/he needs to improve upon and study further. While the questions may be classroom related, others may be on a broader spectrum for a real-world event even outside of the immediate classroom.

Answering these questions correctly will further help with tips for the rest of the exam, which may rely on one concept at a time as opposed to a combination of several at once. However, these questions are neither multiple choice nor short answers. There are also no answers provided, so the test taker will have to do his or her own research to better understand the needs of his/her school community.

Examples:

1. What could foster a quality principal-parent relationship?
2. What resources would help students in preparing for new standardized tests?
3. Why should teacher performance be regularly evaluated?
4. How should state educational laws on education be explained to students and parents?

HOW QUESTIONS AND SCORES ARE DIVIDED?

1. Visions and Goals: 20 percent of exam, 18 multiple choice questions, 2 constructed-response questions
2. Teaching and Learning: 30 percent of exam, 25 multiple choice questions, 3 constructed-response questions
3. Organizational Systems and Safety: 10 percent of exam, 15 multiple choice questions, no constructed-response questions
4. Collaboration with Key Stakeholders: 15 percent of exam, 21 multiple choice questions, no constructed-response question
5. Ethics and Integrity: 15 percent of exam, 21 multiple choice questions, no constructed-response question
6. Education System: 10 percent of exam, no multiple choice question, 2 constructed-response questions

WHAT'S NOT, LEAST, EXCEPT ON THE EXAM?

While this is explored more in the multiple choice question section of the handbook, it's worth reminding test takers that there will be questions that ask for answers to be excluded. To help avoid confusion, all questions that include exclusionary single answers as opposed to multiple incorrect answers, "NOT," "LEAST," and "EXCEPT," will all be in capital letters at the end of each question.

While it is up to the test taker to not overlook these questions, they're formatted this way to help along in the test-taking process.

Sample question 1: For an incoming principal who would like to open the lines of communication with faculty, all of the following steps should be taken EXCEPT

a. encourage teachers to have an "idea" meeting once a month where they can all share new ideas that they think will help improve with classroom participation
b. create an online suggestion box where teachers can submit anonymous tips, complaints, and suggestions to the principal and assistant principal
c. work with teachers to organize an after-work event where faculty members will be encouraged to participate in a fun activity (dance class, craft course)
d. ask teachers to participate in a meeting about what ways the school can continue to have more student participation in classes

The "correct" answer to this question is Choice B. While all of the other answers provide an opportunity for teachers and the principal to get together to discuss student concerns, suggestions, and ideas and get to know each other, anonymous suggestions do not. While this may help the principal learn what the teachers like and don't like or want to change, this also doesn't help with effective, long-term communication.

What is useful about anonymous question boxes (or online systems) is that they give a faculty member the opportunity to be honest and possibly blunter than would be the usual behavior of speaking to someone face-to-face. However, if the principal doesn't know who left the question and needs more information to answer the question, either the person who left the suggestion will eventually have to speak up or the concern will remain unresolved.

The idea of opening communication should be to encourage teachers to come talk directly to the principal, not to each other or to a mysterious box instead.

Some test takers may be curious about Choice C because although it is an opportunity to communicate, faculty members may talk about everything but work. However, in some work environments, being able to speak freely about appropriate personal stories may make employees also to be more receptive to discussing business.

Sample question 2: In 2013, handwriting courses began to dwindle in elementary schools. Instead of learning the alphabet in cursive, students are being encouraged to utilize technology for note-taking. A new student has transferred to a school in the principal's district, and the parent has found out that this school is one of many that has opted out of handwriting.

However, both parents of the child would prefer that the child learn handwriting anyway in an educational setting. The parents schedule a meeting with the principal to encourage the principal to have a change of heart about the course.

If the principal wants to make sure that the parents do not transfer the child elsewhere and continue to utilize the prepared computer courses, which technique should the principal use with parents the LEAST?

a. Explain to the parents that national standards do not require handwriting courses to be taught.
b. Explain the results of why smartphones, laptops, and tablet computers are continuing to gain in popularity from high school to college and graduate school levels, and why making students familiar with these types of technology will help them in later years.
c. Explain the pros of technology courses helping students with typing classes for computers that may have temporarily gone by the wayside as typewriters became less popular.
d. Invite parents to shadow a course in web coding and web programming, using handheld electronics, and utilizing the Internet to show what the educational perks are of investing in this course.

The "correct" answer to this question is Choice A. The other three responses help parents learn how technology may influence their child's education for the future, even past elementary school graduation. While Choices B and C verbally explain why the teachers and principals continue to use these new teaching mechanisms, Choice D goes one step further by inviting parents to see the technology tips in action.

However, Choice A sets the lowest bar for explaining why a school opted out of teaching a course. It also calls into question how many other courses education leadership would drop if national standards gave them the green light to do so. This choice also does not effectively help parents understand the bright side of focusing on technology and why cursive handwriting may not be as useful in today's classrooms.

FILL IN THE CORRECT TEST OPTION

It is extremely important that the SLLA test taker follow along with all instructions that the supervising attendant gives to test takers before the test begins. One of the most important parts is knowing how to use the SLLA computerized test to skip and return to questions.

If the test taker does not know how to reverse to find old questions, he or she runs the risk of leaving them all blank. It will undoubtedly be a disappointment to a test taker to find out that his or her answers could have been correct, but the sections where the answers should have been added were missing or the wrong answer choice was selected.

While this was a common problem with Scan Tron test results, as of January 2012, the SLLA solely offers the exam in a computer-delivered format. However, test takers must still know how to move throughout the software to avoid potential problems more common with paper testing.

The same can be said for constructed-response questions. Say, for example, the test taker has trouble with deciding how to answer Question 103. The test taker moves on to Question 104, however, but does not move to the correct page to start taking notes and writing.

The test scorer will more than likely catch on that the test taker is answering the wrong question. However, if the test taker's response could possibly relate to both questions, this may be less easy to identify. Before filling in any answers on the multiple choice or computerized written notes, double-check the number of the answer area.

Also, double-check other important documentation that will be required to complete the test, including last name, first name, Social Security number, mailing address, telephone number, candidate ID number, test center reporting location, test code/form code, test book serial number, and test name.

In addition to choosing the correct option, make sure the selections are also filled in correctly. One simple error on a Social Security number could slow down the process of notifying the test taker of test results.

IGNORE THE TEST MYTHS

One of the biggest annoyances about myths is how easy it is for people to believe them. The SLLA exam is designed to be as honest and straightforward as possible for all test takers. That means common testing myths do not fit the style of the test:

Tricky words: The phrasing of the questions is not written with tricky language, the questions are reviewed and written with accurate verbiage to resemble the ISLLC standards language. All EXCEPT, NOT, and LEAST questions are designed to be as noticeable as possible to help the test taker in recognizing the unrelated or incorrect response.

Referring to ***sample question 2*** above, and if the test taker felt that there was a trick to the question, the test taker could transition the question into pointing out reasons that handwriting should be taught in the school again. However, the question asked for two other choices to be explored instead: not dropping the pre-pared computer courses and trying to find ways for the parents to continue to want their child to stay at the school.

Answer patterns: The multiple choice answers do not have a pattern or regularly spell out any particular words (e.g., cab for C-A-B).

Duplicate responses: It is possible and probable that multiple choice answers will have similar responses. Finding more than one A, B, C, D, and other selections in a row is not uncommon.

Guessing answers: If the test taker does not know the correct answer, it is OK to guess. While there may be the possibility that the guessed answer will be incorrect, it is better to try to guess from possible correct answers than to leave a question blank altogether.

Writing in the booklet: The test booklet is not what the test taker will be scored on. It is not only allowable but welcomed for test takers to make notes in the booklet to help with any notes, thoughts, unfamiliar and familiar words, or questions that the test taker may have. Just make sure to add any important information to the answer sheets.

The test scorer will not refer to the test booklet to read the final responses. The booklets will be sent to Educational Testing Service (ETS) after the test taker finishes the exam and eventually discarded.

Use the test booklet to take notes that meet the following guidelines:

1. Answer every question.
2. Be able to explain the rationale for that answer.
3. Include professional and subject-specific knowledge to let test scorers know how experienced the test taker is at coming to responses like these, if applicable.
4. Utilize all data that is given to respond to each question.

Before submitting the test answers, and if time permits, the test taker should take a second look through the exam to make sure no questions have been skipped, no blank spaces are left where answers should be, and all notes make sense. Although the order of the responses may not matter so much as effectively answering the question, reread-ing and proofreading answers for grammar and spelling is also a professional touch that may help the test scorer to arrive at an undistracted score, too.

Section 2

Background Information

SLLA is a national testing program used as part of the licensure process for educational leaders. The research included in this test is a combination of the most current professional judgment and experience for educators around the world.

While the passing scores may vary per state, the SLLA test is honored nationwide for teachers and education leaders who may choose to work in another state. The test was designed by ETS using the 2015 Professional Standards for Educational Leaders, formerly known as the ISLLC Standards.

Each license will be used to confirm that a professional in the educational industry, along with many other industries, has sufficiently studied the guidelines to become an effective, safe, and honorable leader within the schooling system. The SLLA exam assures all stakeholders (teachers, parents, and students) that beginning educational leaders are equipped for the industry.

Each state may require its own domain (specified and sometimes localized content) before each professional begins to practice within the educational profession.

The SLLA test was developed by a team. By survey, countrywide education leaders and professors in schools of education were asked their opinions on what qualifications and knowledge a new education leader should have. After the job analysis surveys were complete, the results were ranked by importance. An additional group of administrators reviewed the results.

The original responses and feedback from the job analysis surveys were used to create the multiple choice questions, constructed-response questions, and guidelines to complete the ETS Standards for Quality and Fairness.

Afterward a local faculty panel conducted a validity study to make sure the guidelines, multiple choice questions, and constructed-response questions were valid for their states. A recommended score was then established for new educational leaders to pass the exam per their local markets. Each state's licensing agency confirmed the final score.

This is why the SLLA test may be honored when a teacher transfers from one school to the next but may require additional testing if the score is not high enough for that region.

SUCCESSFUL PASSING SCORES PER STATE

This list of passing SLLA Scores is taken from the ets.org website, make sure that you check here if your state requires the SLLA and what the passing score is[1]. Of note, the states that are not listed, for example Texas and California have their own School Administrator Asssessments so be sure to check the state department of education website of which you will be applying for a position in school administration. The ETS website is: https://www.ets.org/Media/Tests/SLS/pdf/15884passingscores.pdf

SCHOOL LEADERS LICENSURE ASSESSMENT

Arkansas.	163: Building-level administrator, curriculum program administrator
District of Columbia.	163: Administrative services credential
Kansas.	165: Building leadership
Kentucky.	160: Instructional leadership (principal of Grades K–12, Level 1)*
Louisiana	166: Educational leader (Level 1, principals and supervisors)
Maine.	163: Administrator of Special Education, Assistant Administrator of Special Education, Adult and Community Education Director, Building Administrator, Assistant Building Administrator, Curriculum Coordinator
Maryland.	165: Principal, Administrator II
Michigan.	163: Principal
Mississippi.	169: Administrator K–12
Missouri:	No longer eligible to take SLLA exam as of September 1, 2014, and must take the Missouri Educator Gateway Assessments (MEGA) instead
New Jersey.	163: Principal
Pennsylvania.	163: Principal or Vocational Director
Rhode Island.	166: Building-level administrator (Grades P, K–12)
Tennessee.	160: Instructional leadership (Beginning Pre-K–12)
Utah.	163: Administrative and supervisory K–12
Vermont.	163: Assistant Director for Adult Education, Career Technical Director, Curriculum Director, Director of Special Education, Principal, Superintendent
Virginia.	163: Central Office Administrators/Principals

For Kentucky test takers, the Kentucky Specialty Test of Instructional and Administrative Practices is slightly longer with 120 selected response questions, which include 20 pretest questions. SLLA exams in other states are usually 100 multiple choice questions and seven constructed-response questions.

Worldwide locations:

• Guam 163: Initial Administrator Certificate
• U.S. Virgin Islands 156: Principal, Assistant Principal

SLLA TEST TAKERS WHO TRANSFER TO NEW JOBS

For test takers who may later take on job opportunities in a different state, and due to the SLLA being considered a national exam, education professionals can transfer their scores for employment elsewhere. However, because each state does not have the same passing score, there could be a possibility that the test taker must retake the exam if that person's score was not high enough.

Passing test scores in the United States range from 160 to 169, with Mississippi's passing score as the highest.

Education professionals who reside in Missouri should check with transfer locations to find out whether their previous SLLA exam scores (before 2014) are eligible in other states, or if job opportunities in other states will honor the score on the MEGA.

Some states require that test takers have completed the exam within a certain time period[2] although the test scores are available for 10 years. Each test taker should check on both the passing rate and whether that test score is valid by test date standards.

REGISTRATION FEES

While there are no registration fees to take the SLLA exam, there are test fees[3] associated with the exam. If an emergency or conflicting schedule test date occurs, test takers will have the option of rescheduling. However, it must be at least four full days before the registered test exam date. There may be a fee for rescheduling dates.

If a test taker is absent altogether without rescheduling, the testing fee will not be refunded. Nonrefundable fees also include test center change, telephone registration, additional score report per individual request for each report, and score review for SLLA (6011).

On the day of the test, test takers must bring suitable ID in order to enter and complete the SLLA exam, in addition to a printed version of the admissions ticket. While the admissions ticket will be available after the test purchase is complete, test takers are encouraged to verify the admissions ticket a few days before the test date to confirm the check-in information and location.

Admissions tickets will not be mailed to SLLA test takers who registered online. It is the sole responsibility of the test taker to make sure this information is printed out and available to the supervisor at the testing center on the day of the test.

USING THE COMPUTER TO TAKE THE TEST

Each user will receive instructions[4] during the computerized test about how to use the computer interface. Other areas that the test taker will have the chance to review are how to properly answer questions, how to skip questions, how to go back to any questions that were skipped over, and how to properly select multiple choice questions.

USING THE SCHOOL LEADERSHIP SERIES ONLINE ACCOUNT

SLLA test preparers will have the option to select test-related information online for the ordering of the test. That includes:

- Demographic information about the test taker
- Order history for all payments
- Personal information and profile updates
- Print options for the admission ticket to the SLLA exam
- Recipients to receive test scorers
- Registration changes
- Seat reservation
- Scores and additional score reports
- Test center
- Test payments
- Test registration

RESTRICTED ITEMS DURING THE TEST

While every test center may be different, in general, the following items are not allowed into the testing facilities.[5]

- Handbags
- Knapsacks
- Briefcases
- Water bottles
- Canned bottles
- Beverages
- Practice sample test
- Practice sample books
- Practice sample notes
- Calculators (generally not permitted but check per testing location)
- Pens (will be provided at testing center)
- Pencils (will be provided at testing center)
- Scrap paper (will be provided at testing center)
- Electronic devices that record, photograph, or are used as listening devices, outside of medically approved supplies

UNRESTRICTED HEALTH-RELATED ITEMS DURING THE TEST

While every test center may be different, in general, the following items are not allowed in the testing facilities.[6]

- Canes
- Crutches
- Glucose test kit (notify supervisors for permission before the test date)
- Hearing aid
- Heart rate monitor
- Insulin pump (two-part pumps with a transmitter may require additional permission)
- Prosthetic limb
- Service animal
- Voice amplifier

- Walker
- Wheelchair

Before arriving at the testing center, check beforehand to see if the facility has storing units, lockers, or nearby locations to temporarily lock any restricted material. While some facilities do have storage features, none will be held responsible for any lost or stolen items during the time of the test.

TEST TAKERS WITH DISABILITIES

ETS is committed to helping test takers with disabilities or health concerns that will be essential during the exam.

For computer testing, test takers will have the option of using:

- Ergonomic keyboards
- IntelliKeys keyboards
- Screen magnification
- Selectable foreground and background colors for the display monitor
- Touchpad keyboard
- Trackball

Other assistance accommodations will include:

- Braille slate and stylus (for test takers who are visually impaired)
- Oral interpreter (for test takers who are hearing impaired)
- Perkins Brailler (for test takers who are visually impaired)
- Printed copy for spoken directions (for test takers utilizing home-delivery tests)
- Sign language interpreter (for test takers who are hearing impaired)

Additional testing time, a separate room to complete the exam, and extra rest room breaks are also options for test takers who meet the requirements for Americans with Disability Act (ADA).

Test takers should submit any additional requests mentioned above as soon as possible. It may take approximately six weeks for approval from ETS for computer-delivered testing, home-delivered testing, or any alternate testing requests.

All testing accommodations can be sent to:

Mail:

ETS Disability Services
PO Box 6054
Princeton, NJ 08541-6054, USA
Courier Service:
ETS Disability Services
225 Phillips Boulevard

Ewing, NJ 08628-1426, USA
Email: disability.reg@ets.org

AFTER THE TEST IS OVER: READING SCORES

Each Test Taker Score Report will notify test takers if they passed or did not pass for that state, in addition to their numerical score. All scores are readily available after a two- to three-week window from the test date has closed, and they will continue to be available for 10 years afterward.[7]

SLLA test scores are automatically sent to the state department in Arkansas, District of Columbia, Indiana, Kansas, Kentucky, Louisiana, Maryland, Mississippi, Missouri, New Jersey, North Carolina, Pennsylvania, Rhode Island, Tennessee, Utah, and Virginia.

Test takers will also receive their scores sent to the mailing address that was filled out on the beginning pages of the test, in addition to any additional people that the test taker may have paid an additional fee for the test scores to be sent to. The test taker also has the ability and the right to share those test scores with anyone they choose to.

Additional score reports can be made available by request at the online registration site.

Test score documentation will also list additional scores, including:

- Average performance range
- Decision reliability
- Median
- Passing score
- Possible score range
- Raw points (ratings assigned by test scorers)
- Reliability (consistency of test scorers across each test section)
- Scaled score (calculation of difficulty of test form administered plus the raw score)
- Score interval
- Standard error of measurement (statistic calculating the error liability of test scorers)
- Standard error of scoring (statistic for how often different test scorers will give different scores for the same test taker)
- Validity

Because the test questions may vary from simple to difficult, depending on the test taker and the questions created for the test, ETS is aware that the level of difficulty for all is not possible. For test takers who find themselves answering more detailed or difficult questions, equating is used to adjust for difficulty.

To make the score readability more simple, ETS is transparent about unadjusted[8] and adjusted scores. The unadjusted scores are the raw scores. Adjusted scores are scaled scores. The more difficult the test is, the more likely it is that the test will require less questions that must be correct in order to pass.

Section 3

How the SLLA Is Scored

GRADING ESSAY: CONSTRUCTED-RESPONSE ANSWERS

In the essay portion of the SLLA exam, each of the seven answers will be rated on a 1–3 score basis by the test scorer.

Each question will be broken down into seven categories.

- Implementation of Vision and Goals
- Data Planning
- Building a Professional Culture
- Curriculum and Instruction
- Assessment and Accountability
- Advocacy—Internal
- Advocacy—External

A score of 3 means the test taker has a thorough understanding of the question and created an answer to reflect this.

A score of 2 means the test taker has a basic or general understanding of the question and created an answer to reflect this.

A score of 1 means the test taker has a limited understanding of the question and created an answer to reflect this.

A score of zero (0) means the test taker has little to no understanding of the question and created an answer to reflect this.

In each section, the test scorer will evaluate:

1. How well the test taker's responses reflect each section (e.g., the ability to use multiple sources to analyze and develop shared commitments for the Data Planning section)
2. Whether the test taker has a strong knowledge of each of the seven categories

3. If he or she can explain how to implement strategies from each of the seven categories
4. If he or she can keep each answer relevant for each of the seven categories
5. Whether all answers are in logical, sequential order (e.g., outlines, steps) for each of the seven categories
6. If the test taker can provide logical, reasonable rationales that relate to each question and fully explain the answer for each of the seven categories.

TOPIC MATTER THEMES FROM EACH OF SEVEN CATEGORIES

1: Implementation of Vision and Goals

- Shared commitments
- Motivational speaking/initiatives
- Team building
- Implement strategies
- Communication and group processes

2: Data Planning

- Analyze data systems
- Research for school improvement
- Align planning and resources
- Monitor evidence for ongoing improvement

3: Building a Professional Culture

- Make sure all faculty members stay professional on the job
- Require high standards for all students
- Close achievement gaps
- Communicate with groups

4: Curriculum and Instruction

- Align curriculum with student assessment
- Program evaluation
- Use research and data to close achievement gaps

5: Assessment and Accountability

- Accountability for students and teachers
- Analyze data for student's grades, performance
- Evaluate teaching habits
- Support teachers in classroom assessments

6: Advocacy—Internal

- Embracing and initiating constructive conversations about various factors in an educational environment (e.g., local and national laws, policies, regulations, requirements)

- Develop relationships with stakeholders (parents, faculty members, bus drivers, teachers) to explore and improve on education
- Encourage students and the parents of students to work with faculty and other stakeholders to create equal, shared goals to benefit the students
- Emphasize healthy, professional relationships between all students and faculty members
- Persuade parents to keep open communication with teachers and vice versa

7: Advocacy—External

- Improve on decision making
- Better educational policies within the school environment
- Make sure all stakeholders understand local, state, and federal laws and why these affect everyday life at school
- Make sure all students and stakeholders strive for excellence in learning for everyone involved
- Create strategic alliances to help with a more stable, educational environment

UNDERSTANDING THE TEST SCORERS

While multiple choice questions are graded, the essay questions are more involved. For this reason, even the test scorers must also undergo testing before being granted the rights to be on the ETS team.

Constructed-response questions and answers (essay questions) are scanned into the Online Scoring Network (OSN), which is an electronic virtual scoring system. All tests are scored in a five-or-more-day period. Test scorers are given the option to work from home or in their own offices on an individual basis.

A scoring leader is also assigned to each group for assistance, as a guide and to possibly step in should a test score become questionable. All members of ETS are experienced education leaders or leader educators. In order to qualify to be a scoring leader, the representative must be savvy with scoring SLLA exams already and be able to train and mentor test scorers.

New test scorers are consistently added throughout each testing session to ensure fresh faces and fresh visions and to help with the workload so veteran test scorers (or those who are voluntarily or involuntarily no longer test scorers) do not get boggled down with incoming SLLA test score projects.

KNOWING THE TEST SCORER HAS BEEN PROPERLY TRAINED

For SLLA test takers who wonder who the scorers are behind their exams, they have been properly vetted as well. There are several steps that a test scorer must take in order to be officiated into the program of grading SLLA exams.

- Review an online tutorial (e.g., guidelines, practice scoring)
- Pass a certification test, which includes preapproved questions and responses

• Pass a calibration test, which has prescored responses
• Test results are reviewed by a "super scoring leader" (scoring director) along with test development professionals

After the test scorer has passed the certification test and calibration test, the test scorer is set to start on reviewing SLLA exams for the session.

Knowing how test scorers went about giving test takers their scores of 1–3 matters for two reasons: it will help the test scorer understand where that person went right or wrong, and it will also help the test taker evaluate his or her own scores during the sample test.

During the studying process, test takers can formulate their own responses to the constructed-response questions. Then use the scoring system (rubric) to score those same answers.

Test buddies can then exchange their own answers and grade each other. This will help test takers evaluate their best and poorest points while completing timed written responses. Be just as interested in reviewing the scores of 1 or 2 as the test taker would with a 3, so come test day, the test taker can keep those tips as mental notes.

QUALITY CONTROL FOR ALL TESTS

All of the test takers' answers will be reviewed by two separate test scorers. Each will rank the answers on a 1–3 scale. However, the second scorer cannot see the first scorer's rankings, to eliminate bias.

Once both scorers have calculated their individual results, each test is examined to make sure that the test scorers closely align. If the two test scorers give scores that are the same or one point apart, all scores are added together and the sum of the two scores will be the test takers final grade.

If the test scorers' results are more than one point apart, a scoring leader than grades the test taker's responses a third time without being able to see the first and second scorers' scores. If the results of the scoring leader closely aligns with the results of the first two test scorers, the test scorer will use the sum of the two scores.

However, if the scoring leader's results are more than one score off from the first two, then the scoring leader's numerical results are added onto whichever test scorer's results line up the most with the third set of scores.

RANDOM TESTING OF TEST TAKERS BY SCORE LEADERS

The score leader has the right and the ability to test the score takers at any time. During random testing, if the score leader finds that the test taker is not following the required guidelines for scoring on more than one occasion, the score leader will also grade some of the test scorer's grading results. The score leader will then go over the differing results with the test scorer.

If the problem persists, the test scorer will be removed from the grading team.

The time it takes for a test scorer to evaluate an answer will also be monitored. While not every test scorer will take the same amount of time to evaluate a score, this technique is said to help accuracy.

Test takers will be assured that there will be several test scorers looking at their work, which should lead to a diverse response to help avoid bias. Having a variety of scorers also helps to make testing fair for test scorers who may be more lenient or more strict than others, in order to continue to create a fair environment for the test taker.

OTHER TIPS TO KEEP IN MIND FOR SCORING

While the test scorers and scoring leaders will do their best to provide unbiased, fair, and useful feedback and scoring rates, the test taker should also keep these points in mind while completing the test.

Tip 1: Read the Whole Question: Take No Shortcuts.

While the test taker may be paying attention to the allotted time for each question, try to avoid skipping over valuable information in order to successfully answer part of the question. All answers should be in a cohesive, clear state. If the test scorer has to look around for parts of answer that were never there to begin with, that will hinder the test taker's grade.

Tip 2: Be Organized.

Whether using a numbered list, a bulleted list, an em dash list, or any other kind of list that needs to be used in order to come to a final conclusion, the test takers should try to keep all notes and final answers in a neat, sequential order.

Tip 3: Stay Consistent.

If one set of answers uses roman numerals to complete a point and the next uses Arabic numbers, this could lead to unnecessary confusion. Even if only working on scratch paper, try to follow the usual outlining format: roman numeral first, capital letter second, lowercase "i" series third, and lowercase letters fourth.

Although this system exactly is not required in order to respond to the question, whatever style the test taker chooses, just keep it consistent throughout the post so as not to distract the test taker from the actual answers as opposed to the random way they are displayed.

Tip 4: Justify Your Answer: Know What Will Not Be Known.

Every test taker is not going to understand and be able to explain every answer. There may be a question or two that leaves test takers scratching their heads wondering where was this in the sample guide or textbook or manuals. While anxiety may certainly crop up in the average test taker, try to answer as much as possible of the question even if it's unfamiliar. If that means getting a test score of 1 or 2 instead of 3 for partially answering the question, that is much better than leaving the answer blank altogether.

Tip 5: Avoid Typos.

While SpellCheck and self-editing are useful tools to make sure that the writing of anything is OK, there may be typos and misspellings that creep their way into the writing and editing process anyway. Even an editor needs an editor, so the test taker should not feel immediately discouraged by a word or two. However, as is one of the biggest problems with self-editing, writers tend to imagine that a misspelled word is correct after looking at the same responses for so long.

If the test taker is given the opportunity to take a break, do so. Maybe step back from one of the questions and move onto another question. Then go back and proof the first one. It's awfully surprising how much better the distracted, anxious eye can be when it has the opportunity to rest.

If the test taker cannot move onto the next question without fully understanding the previous one, try looking off into the distance for a few seconds, breathing in and out, and then going back to look at the post.

Tip 6: Reread the Checklist.

The test taker should jot down any notes, questions, concerns, and policies that need to be answered while arriving at the final results of the question.

Refer to "How to approach the essay or the constructed-response questions" for more detailed information on this.

These notes are usually the first ones to come to mind while reading each part of the list. They're like a To Do list. And as with any To Do list, they should be revisited and crossed off as the tasks are complete. Make sure that no tips, queries, or necessary policies were skipped over to jump to the conclusion of the question.

If the answer is written in the kind of chart usually used for Pros and Cons, make sure each step and next answer mirrors the question. If any questions are left unanswered, the test taker should evaluate that answer. Was the original question necessary? Or was it just a random thought or off topic from the end response?

If it's the latter conclusion, move on. If the original checklist response is now confusing or the test taker is wondering why that question or point came up in the first place, don't underestimate those first thoughts. Go back to the question. Reread the full question. Then look at that perplexing comment again. Is it still irrelevant? If so, remove it. If not, proceed with answering it.

This is where the biggest differences are between multiple choice questions and essay questions. With multiple choice questions, the test taker must arrive at the conclusion that one of the given answers is correct. With constructed-response questions, the test taker may have more control in explaining to the test scorer why an answer should be considered.

Tip 7: Do Not Let the Difficulty of Individual Test Scores Be a Distraction.

On the final scoring system, there will be a section for raw-to-scale conversion table, which will take into account the difficulty level of each question. Because there is no way to level out each test so that every multiple choice or constructed-response answer has the same amount of difficulty, in the final scores, the raw scores (actual scores that the test scorers gave each test taker) with the scaled scores (level of difficulty factored into how many must be correct in order to pass the exam).

For Kentucky only:

However, test takers should not assume that since some questions are more difficult than others, the test will be lenient. Kentucky, for example, has 120 multiple choice questions instead of most other states that have 100 questions. However, 20 of the pre-test scores for that state are either correct or incorrect. The scaled score is computed from the raw score.

Tip 8: Make Sure to Let Test Supervisors Know If Extra Assistance Is Needed.

Whether it's extra bathroom breaks, keyboard issues, vision concerns, not being able to hear the opening instructions, or any other health-related issue, this should be covered beforehand. During the registration process, test takers are given the opportunity to explain any health-related causes that could somehow affect their exam.

From diabetic concerns (e.g., insulin allowed in the testing facility) to visual- or hearing-impaired supplies that may be needed during the exam, test takers should be honest about this before launching off into the test. While studying, being awake and properly nourished are necessary for all exams; do not let an easily avoidable health-related cause. hinder the final results.

Refer to "the Background Information" section for more details.

Section 4

Summary of 2015 ISLLC Standards

Take the time to read the 2015 ISLLC Standards and understand what the standards are saying to future school leaders. Really learn the content of the standards and emulate the language associated with the standards.

One key to successful performance on the test is an understanding of the types of knowledge and performance identified by the ISLLC Standards for School Leaders. The assessment and scoring guides were developed to measure whether you possess knowledge relevant to the standards. Therefore, your responses should be guided by a clear understanding of how the ISLLC Standards define school leadership. This knowledge, combined with an understanding of the assessment and what is expected of you—that is, the test content, the types of questions you will encounter, and the types of responses you will be asked to offer—should enhance your confidence in your ability to demonstrate your knowledge and skills.

The National Policy Board for Educational Administration, which writes and revises the national standards for school leaders, explains that the new standards have a forward-thinking outlook. The new standards are inspiring and lead to understanding that the world as we reside in it is ever changing and global in context and expectation. These standards focus on future issues and challenges face by school administrators that encourage academic success throughout the school environment. These future leaders need to be transformative, informed, and ones that encourage and sustain involvement in order to envision a school in which the diverse culture of all is respected and included throughout the school environment.[1]

The 2015 Standards are aspirational in other ways, too. They challenge the profession, professional associations, policy makers, institutions of higher education, and other organizations that support educational leaders and their development to move beyond established practices and systems and to strive for a better future. The 2015 Standards focus on accomplished leadership practice to inspire educational leaders to stretch themselves and reach a level of excellence in their practice, no matter where they are in their careers. They are relevant at all career stages, although application will vary and is an area that the field should explore further.

In this section you will have the most important words associated with each standard. These are the words used in the ISLLC Standards, these are the words used for analyzing the standards. Make index cards and memorize the words of the standards; that way you will be able to write the constructed-response answers using these words. I encourage my students to carry the index cards everywhere they go; that way, whenever they have time, they glance at them. Therefore, making memorizing the standards easier and faster.

You can create electronic index cards, resembling flash cards online for free as well. Below are two helpful websites for creating your own flashcards:

Kitzkikz (http://www.kitzkikz.com/flashcards/) provides a free printable flashcard maker for you to create your own flashcards and study aids. Then you just print, cut, fold, and study.

Quizlet (https://quizlet.com/) is free and lets you take your electronic flashcards everywhere. The website allows you to study the cards using games that Quizlet makes for your flashcards. You can also download the flashcards onto your phone.

STANDARD 1
Mission, Vision, and Core Values
Effective educational leaders develop, advocate, and enact a shared mission, vision, and core values of high-quality education and academic success and well-being of each student.
Vocabulary Associated with Standard 1
Facilitation Challenges Strategic Planning Leadership Capacity Stakeholder Involvement Collaborative Develop and Implement Collect data Assess effectiveness Promote learning Continuous and Sustainable improvement Monitor and Evaluate Modeling the vision

STANDARD 2
Ethics and Professional Norms
Effective educational leaders act ethically and according to professional norms to promote each student's academic success and well-being.
Vocabulary Associated with Standard 2
Integrity, Fairness, Ethics System of accountability Academic and Social success Self-awareness Reflective practice Transparency Ethical Behavior Values of democracy Evaluate potential moral and legal consequences Promote social justice Meet individual student needs Decision quality

Figure 4.1 "ISLLC Standards"

STANDARD 3
Equity and Cultural Responsiveness
Effective educational leaders strive for equity of educational opportunity and culturally responsive practices to promote each student's academic success and well-being.
Vocabulary Associated with Standard 3
Fair Respect Value Diversity Positive Unbiased Global Society Responsiveness Competence Responsiveness Race Class Language Culture Gender Sexual Orientation Disability Special Status Social Economic Advocate for Children, Families, Caregivers Assess and Analyze Anticipate Trends Open Dialogue Communication Assess Interests and Needs Build and Sustain Positive Relationships Build and Sustain Productive Relationships Utilize Community Resources Collaboration Collect and Analyze Data Promote Understanding, Appreciation of Diversity

Figure 4.1   "ISLLC Standards" (Continued)

STANDARD 4
Curriculum, Instruction, and Assessment
Effective educational leaders develop and support intellectually rigorous and coherent systems of curriculum, instruction, and assessment to promote each student's academic success and well-being.
Vocabulary Associated with Standard 4

School Culture	Ensure Mission, Vision, and Core Values
Instructional Program	Align Standards
Student Learning	Culturally Responsive Standards
Professional Growth	Promote Student Academic Success
Climate	Encourage Love of Learning
Nurture and Sustain	Identify Habits of Learners
High Expectation	Encourage Healthy Sense of Self
Comprehensive, Rigorous	Ensure Best Practices
Motivating Learning Environment	Provide Consistent Knowledge
Supervision	Develop Effective Pedagogy
Assessment and Accountability Systems	Meet Student Needs
Monitor Progress	Ensure Instructional Practice
Leadership Capacity	Intellectually Challenging
Quality Instruction	Authentic Learning and Experiences
Technologies	Recognizes Student Strengths
Change	Differentiated and Personalized Instruction
Emerging Issues and Trends	Promote Technology
Involve Stakeholders	Employ Valid Assessments
School Decision-making Process	Develop Technical Standards of Measurement
Visibility	Use Assessment Data
Promote Instructional Practice	Monitor Student Progress
Implement Coherent Curriculum	Improve Instruction
Promote Assessment	

Figure 4.1 "ISLLC Standards" (Continued)

STANDARD 5
Community of Care and Support for Students
Effective educational leaders cultivate an inclusive, caring, and supportive school community that promotes the academic success and well-being of each student.
Vocabulary Associated with Standard 5
Build Safe School Environment Caring Healthy Maintain Physical Atmosphere Support Academics Maintain Social and Emotional Environment Cultivate Student Engagement Sustain Trusted Environment Accepted, Valued, Respected, Cared For Encourage Responsibility Infuse Cultures and Languages of School Community Know Students Understand Community Needs Support Adult-Student Relationships Reinforce Student Engagement Positive Development Infuse School Culture into Learning Impart Academic Values of Learning

Figure 4.1   "ISLLC Standards" (Continued)

STANDARD 6
Professional Capacity of School Personnel
Effective educational leaders develop the professional capacity and practice of school personnel to promote each student's academic success and well-being.
Vocabulary Associated with Standard 6
Provides Services Writing, Reviewing, Implementing Services Quality Effective Recruit, Hire, Support, Develop, Retain Staff Manage Staff Turnover Succession Provide Opportunities Mentoring Personnel Guided Professional Development Differentiated Learning Professional Growth Foster Continuous Improvement Outcomes Based Deliver Feedback Professional Practice Research-anchored Evaluation Support Knowledge, Skills, and Practice Empower Staff Continuous Learning Develop Teacher Leadership Promote Professional Health Well-being Maintain Healthy Work-Life balance Promote Reflection, Study, Improvement

Figure 4.1 "ISLLC Standards" (Continued)

STANDARD 7
Professional Community for Teachers and Staff
Effective educational leaders foster a professional community of teachers and other professional staff to promote each student's academic success and well-being.
Vocabulary Associated with Standard 7
Develop Workplace Conditions Meet Academic, Social, Emotional, and Physical Needs Establish Culture of Engagement Commitment to Shared Vision and Objectives Whole Child High Expectations Professional Work Ethical and Equitable Practice Culture of Trust Open Communication Collaboration Collective Efficacy Continuous Learning Promote Accountability for Student Success School Effectiveness Develop Trusting Working Relationships Support Open, Productive, Caring Relationships Promote Professional Capacity Culture of Improvement Design Professional Learning Implement Professional Opportunities Provide Collaborative Opportunities Examination of Practice Collegial Feedback Collective Learning Faculty initiated Encourage Improvement

Figure 4.1   "ISLLC Standards" (Continued)

STANDARD 8
Meaningful Engagement of Families and Community
Effective educational leaders engage families and the community in meaningful, reciprocal, and mutually beneficial ways to promote each student's academic success and well-being.
Vocabulary Associated with Standard 8

Value Diversity	Understand Strengths
Assess Interests and Needs	Communicate Needs
Utilize Community Resources	Develop Productive Relationships
Collaboration	Engage School Community
Collect and Analyze Data	Partner with Families
Promote Understanding, Appreciation	Support Student Learning
of Diversity	Value Culture
Build and Sustain Positive Relationships	Integrate Community
Build and Sustain Productive	Employ Community Resources
Relationships	Cultural
Emerging Issues and Trends	Social
Involve Stakeholders	Intellectual
School Decision-making Process	Political
Visibility	Develop Resources
Approachable	Provide School Resources
Accessible	Advocate School Needs
Welcoming	School Priorities
Create Positive Relationships	Advocate for Students, Families, and
Sustain Relationships	Community
Collaborative Community	Build Productive Partnerships
Engage in Communication	Promote School Improvement
Open Two-way	
Maintain Community Presence	

Figure 4.1 "ISLLC Standards" (Continued)

STANDARD 9	
Operations and Management	
Effective educational leaders manage school operations and resources to promote each student's academic success and well-being.	
Vocabulary Associated with Standard 9	
Coordinating	Responsible for Nonmonetary
Organizing	Resources
Planning	Accountable
Resource Acquisition and Management	Ethical Management
Ensure Safety	Effective Budgeting
Monitor, Evaluate Management and	Accounting Practices
Operations	Protect Learning Disruptions
Obtain, Allocate, Utilize	Employ Technology
Promote and Protect	Improve Quality
Distributive Leadership	Efficiency of Operations
Support Quality Instruction	Maintain Data Systems
Consensus Building	Deliver Actionable Information
Quality Personnel	Develop Data-driven School
Institute Procedures	Improvement
Manage Operations	Know Laws, Rights, Policies, and
Monitor Processes	Regulations
Promote Systematic Mission and Vision	Promote Student Success
of School	Know Local, State, and Federal Laws
Manage Resources	Manage Feeder and Connecting Schools
Assign Roles	Understand Student Enrolment
Proper Implementation of Scheduling	Manage Curricular Articulation
Optimize Professional Capacity	Develop Central Office Relationships
Allocate Responsibility	Sustain School Board Relationships
Manage Fiscal Resources	Administer Fair and Equitable Conflict
Support Curriculum	Management
Professional Capacity	Manage Governance Processes
Community Engagement	Adhere to Internal and External Politics
Stewards of Monetary Resources	Focus on School Vision and Mission

Figure 4.1 "ISLLC Standards" (Continued)

STANDARD 10	
School Improvement	
Effective educational leaders act as agents of continuous improvement to promote each student's academic success and well-being.	
Vocabulary Associated with Standard 10	
Make School Effective	Evaluate Research for School Improvement
Continuous Improvement	Develop Data Collection
Achieve School Vision	Data Analysis and Management
Fulfill School Mission	District Office
Promote Core School Values	External Partners for Support
Prepare School Improvement	Planning
Promoting Readiness	Implementation
Instill Mutual Commitment	Monitoring, Feedback, and Evaluation
Accountability	Adopt Systems Perspective
Develop Knowledge	Promote Coherence for Improvement
Increase Skills	Encourage School Programs
Motivate Success	Support School Services
Seek Improvement	Manage Uncertainty
Engage Others in an Ongoing Process	Risk
Evidence-based Inquiry	Competing Initiatives
Continuous Learning	Politics of Change
Strategic Goal Setting	Courage and Perseverance
Planning	Provide Resources
Implementation	Provide Encouragement
Evaluation	Openly Communicate
School Improvement	Outcomes Processes
Employ Improvement Strategies	Develop Leadership
Situationally Appropriate Improvement	Support Teachers and Staff
Transformational	Encourage Inquiry
Incremental	Promote Experimentation
Adaptive Approaches	Implement Innovation
Develop Staff	Initiating Improvement
Assess Applicability of Educational Trends	

Part II

GUIDELINES FOR SUCCESS

Section 5

Guidelines for SLLA Success

Given that the SLLA is considered by many schools and state departments of education to be the most accurate measure of your ability to perform in a school as an aspiring principal, it is given a tremendous amount of weight in the certification process. So, it's important to invest significant time and energy prior to taking the SLLA.

Use these guidelines to get started:

1. ***It's a marathon, not a sprint***. Oftentimes aspiring principals will let SLLA preparation slip by the wayside during their busy weeks in school or at work, only to spend hours on the weekends cramming and taking an endless number of practice tests. While practice tests are important, it's best to keep your mind SLLA ready at all times, practicing a new section each day with the occasional or weekly practice test thrown in the mix, experts say. Andrew Brody, national content director for the Princeton Review, compares preparing for standardized exams to training for a marathon. Brody encourages students to keep their minds sharp at all times, but not to overwork them. Brody explains, "You wouldn't run a marathon every day to train for a marathon." "But you also wouldn't do nothing all week and then run miles and miles on the weekend. You do a little bit of focused work [everyday] to keep yourself in shape with occasional long runs—or practice tests—mixed in." It is grueling work, studying, but you have to keep a steady pace at it. This is not a race, it is for comprehension of material that is provided for you here in this book.

2. ***Creating a study schedule***. Make an appointment with yourself, for example, every Saturday from 9:00 am to noon or every Tuesday and Thursday from 5:00 pm to 7:00 pm when your classes are over. And do not schedule anything else for that period of time. This creates a study routine. Make your scheduled study time as if you have an important meeting or a doctor's appointment. Or as if you have to go to work at that designated time; this creates a consistent study schedule that you will not break and good study habits. Understand that you do not compromise your study time for anything else.

3. ***Study time***. The second important consideration in creating your plan is to honestly assess how much time you are willing to spend on studying. Some test

takers can adopt to an intense study regime because, despite working in a normal full-time position in a school setting, these test takers are willing to consistently carve out 10–12 hours a week to devote to SLLA preparation. This method is not for everyone. Many students are very busy; naturally they are busy because of their work, travel, and families. As you develop a plan for test preparation, be honest with yourself. How much time will you have each week to commit to SLLA prep? Can you find a quiet place to sit for four hours and take a practice test? Just like going to the gym, you will see results only when you have been brutally honest with yourself and are unwilling to compromise. This may be where study groups come in: They can force you to meet once or twice a week for months.

4. ***Study space***. You need to find an uninterrupted place where to study. If your university library is not open during the study time that you have set aside for yourself, find another location. There is the student center on campus frequently open for long hours; find a corner on a different level than the first floor to study. The public library and other university or college libraries are also available and commonly allow other students to study within their spaces. Cafes, like Panera, McDonald's, or local cafes, typically open early and close late. There are usually quiet places within these locations that provide for a study space. Understanding and implementing successful study strategies is key to passing this exam for certification.

5. ***Group study starts here***. There are benefits to studying anything with a friend; the SLLA exposes your personal strengths and weaknesses more clearly than other standardized tests, experts say. Given the analytic nature of most questions, what comes easily to one person may prove to be a challenge for the study partner. Studying in a group can be beneficial, given that it might make you prone to review the test in a general fashion rather than focusing on your specific weaknesses. Studying in a group gives different perspectives for resolving each constructed-response essay question on the SLLA. Each group member has different qualities or ideas to offer to the study group. Studying by yourself will always get you one perspective; yet, in groups, you may receive various viewpoints which can assist you to reach your own conclusions. Listening and asking questions will provide more food for thought developing your critical skills or the standards that you might have missed in answering that essay question.

6. ***Does Away with Procrastination***. The SLLA exam, which is a four-hour exam, is not one that a test taker should procrastinate studying for. There is a great deal of complexity associated with this exam. Many students tend to cram for exams on the week or weekend before or begin studying with very limited time before the due date. If you are one of those students, it is not too late to seek out classmates who are taking this exam or ask around in your building if any of your colleagues will be taking this exam and create a study group. When in a study group, meeting at scheduled times can keep the active participants from procrastinating. In addition, individuals in study groups are less likely to delay or put off study sessions because they understand that other people are relying on them.

7. ***Engages Information and Understands Efficiently***. Students tend to learn faster working within a group versus working alone. If a student was working on his/her own, there would be a lot of time wasted trying to unravel the scenario provided

on the practice SLLA. However, when students work in groups, they have the opportunity to explain concepts, review material, exchange ideas, and disagree or reason with one another about why one person's answer differs from another. Therefore, one can seek clarification and learn faster working in a group setting while gaining personal skills.

8. *Know the content: The standards*. Because the SLLA does not quiz you on content but rather how you use judgment and think analytically, cramming with a colleague or classmate is of little benefit. It's best to learn what gives you the most trouble and drill yourself on those questions alone or with the help of a study partner. The questions at the end of this book are given the ISLLC Standard associated with it so as to help you better understand your weakness areas. Because the SLLA is a skills-based test, "every student is unique," says Jeff Thomas, director of programs at Kaplan Test Prep and Admissions. "If a student and a buddy are prepping for an exam and if they go along the same course of action, same assignments, same prep exercises, they're going to have immensely different results. Every student is different."

9. *Answer everything*. Unlike the SAT, there is no penalty for getting an incorrect answer on the SLLA, so it's important to at the very least make an educated guess on each question. Leaving it blank does you no good. Also, every question is weighted the same. Tougher questions count just the same toward the final score as their simpler counterparts, so don't get bogged down trying to answer the difficult ones. Answer as many easy questions as you can and revisit the tough questions with your remaining time. It's much wiser to tackle questions that are in your wheelhouse first and guess on the harder ones than to dwell on the difficult ones and rush through simpler ones as your time expires, potentially botching them because of the time crunch. "The questions that you spend the most time on are the ones you're most likely to get wrong," says Goehring. "Even if you were guaranteed to get the question right, but you had to spend five minutes on it, how many easy questions would you have gotten right in that same amount of time?"[1]

10. *Get motivated*. Find a way to pump yourself up for exam day. A positive, optimistic, enthusiastic attitude toward the exam will inspire you to work hard and stay focused during the last couple weeks before you take the SLLA. The SLLA can be tedious, so find something to inspire and motivate you.

11. *Stay healthy*. The stress of the last weeks before taking the SLLA can take a toll on your body and mind. Make sure that you eat healthy, avoid drinking alcohol, and exercise or at least take a short walk daily. Don't pull all-nighters and be sure to get plenty of sleep every night. You want to be awake, aware, focused, and feeling great when you walk into the test center.

12. *Exam materials*. Prepare a ziplock bag with your admissions ticket, ID, photograph, and medical products. You don't want to forget anything, so make sure that you have this ready in advance. Make a checklist and double-check the bag before you go to bed the night before the exam to make sure that everything is there.

13. *Minimize test anxiety*. Test anxiety is an uneasiness experienced before, during, or after an examination because of concern, worry, or fear. Some students find that anxiety interferes with their learning and test-taking to such an extent that their grades are seriously affected. Being able to recognize anxiety and create a

group with motivated colleagues or classmates is often helpful. Instructors agree that studying with others improve student performance on standardized exams and assignments.

14. ***Retake practice tests***. Take the practice tests at the end of this book multiple times. That way you are familiar with the testing language and expectations. Take them over and over until you are too familiar with them. You must review all the questions that you got wrong in order to know what and how to improve. The explanations of the answers are extremely valuable in teaching you whatever ISLLC Standards that you are lacking an understanding of.

Section 6

How to Approach the
Multiple Choice Questions

The tricky part about multiple choice questions is that not only the answers will vary for each question, but there could be two or more points that seem to be correct even if one of the choices isn't "All of the Above." And if none of the answers seem to be correct and there is no option for "None of the Above," then that's another issue entirely.

Here are a few tips to avoid losing time on the clock and obsessing over an answer to a multiple choice question.

Tip 1: For answers that the test taker is sure are right, answer those questions immediately.

Nothing will stress a test taker out more than noticing easy questions that were left blank because time ran out. Get through those multiple choice questions that the test taker knows like the back of his or her hand first. Mark the ones that puzzle the test taker so it's easier to scope them out again later, but just keep pushing through.

Example:
A parent joins the Parent-Teacher Associations (PTA) board and would like to know why the assistant principal is not relaying messages back to the principal. What should the principal do first?

1. Assure the parent that all discussions are being passed along, as instructed.
2. Consult the assistant principal about what concerns the parent feels are not being passed along.
3. Since the assistant principal was given authority by the principal to act on the principal's behalf, explain this to the parent.
4. Schedule a discussion between the parent and the assistant principal to find out what concerns the parent have.

As with any professional in a work atmosphere, the first thing to do before taking any disciplinary action or assuming that something is being worked on is to ask first.

If the message managed to get to the principal, then the parent was clearly being persistent about wanting to get the issues to the highest authority.

However, the assistant principal should also have the opportunity to share whether those ideas were or were not shared. There could be a number of possibilities of why some messages may have gotten lost in travel: upcoming meetings that haven't happened yet or canceled meetings, or the issue resolved through other stakeholders that did not need the principal's input to carry out.

Option 4 gives both the parent and the assistant principal an opportunity to explain what was and was not shared, whether those situations in the PTA meeting were resolved, and whether there were any additional concerns that needed to be aired out.

Tip 2: Count off the questions that remain unanswered.

This may seem obvious, but when taking an exam that has multiple sections, it's easy to overlook a question and think either it has already been answered or it was never read to begin with. Whether it's an asterisk, an exclamation mark, or any other noticeable symbol, make sure those blank answers can be found again from a quick fan breeze through the pages.

Tip 3: Reread the question to see if it really is that difficult.

It's possible that the question that used to seem awfully difficult before is now obvious. But why? One reason may be the stress load of trying to get through the exam. Just as people sometimes "go blank" over commonly used words, the same can be said of an exam. If the questions and answers seem easier, take another run through those marked questions, reread them, and answer as efficiently as possible.

Tip 4: Use the third round for the most challenging questions.

These questions are usually ones with answers that the test taker thinks should be "All of the Above" or "None of the Above," or should have multiple answers, but the combination of "A and B" or "B and D" just aren't options to choose from. Reread the question. Make sure that whatever the answers are that the test taker is stumbling over actually answer the question asked, have no inaccurate information in them, and meet the theme of that section of the test.

Tip 5: When it's right, it's right.

Revisiting those answers that could be "All of the Above" or the test taker is extremely confident in one of the choices, here's another way to narrow down whether an answer should be chosen. If no other response has what the test taker believes is the correct answer, choose it.

For example, say all of the questions have more than one response for the answer in each choice (e.g., II and III or B and C). If "B" or "II" is absolutely correct, but the test taker is unsure about the second response, do not sway away from the test taker's first mind about the correct answer, thinking, "Well, I'm not so sure that III (or C) is correct so I'll look at I and IV (or A and D) instead."

While the creator of the test may not be intending to trip up the test taker, that's exactly what's happening. This is one of those questions to mark and revisit later. Don't choose a completely wrong answer just because one of the alternatives is stumping the test taker.

Tip 6: Be careful with negatively worded questions.

Do not be in such a hurry to respond to a question that the test taker doesn't pay attention to what the question is trying to eliminate. Instead of asking what may be the most correct choice, a question may ask which of the choices is *not* correct. Questions like this can be a real forehead smacker later on down the line if the test taker realizes after the test is complete that the question wasn't understood.

While reading the entire blurb for the question, make sure to take a second glance at the actual question as opposed to assuming what the question will be. This is equally important for True or False questions. Sometimes the test may ask which answer is valid and which one isn't.

Tip 7: Know what all key terms mean beforehand.

There is no better friend to a student than an online or print dictionary. Or, maybe, it's a textbook that explains a key term in full detail. Always look up any unfamiliar words, confusing policies, and perplexing "correct" answers in the study guide and anything else that could stump a test taker.

It is one thing to not know which answer is correct from a possibility of numerous correct answers or no correct answers. However, there's another level of disappointment in not even being familiar with the question to begin with.

For example, say a law or a person's job title is mentioned in a question asking how a principal should proceed in a legal battle. If the test taker doesn't have any idea of what the legal cases, legal terms, or policy language means, it's going to all look like gibberish.

Treat unfamiliar test-taking topics the same way dictionary subscribers treat a Word of the Day. Whether through flash cards, notes, or rereading content over again, get comfortable with speaking about *just* that topic on its own even without answering the question.

The more a test taker knows about the background of a policy and what it means, the more confident the test taker will be in narrowing down which answers couldn't work for a particular question.

Example:
A parent arrives to a school to complain about the school cafeteria's lunch. Her child is extremely allergic to nuts. The mother would prefer that nuts not be served anywhere near her child's lunch and threatens to sue the school if any health issues occur due to his allergies. What should the principal do in this situation?

a. Explain to the parent that lunches cannot be changed due to one child's individual
    health issues. Suggest that the child bring an EpiPen if a sudden allergic reaction
    happens while on the school premises.
b. Offer an option for the child to complete schoolwork from home on approved days
    to avoid the child's attendance rate decreasing on days when the school menu may
    contain nut food choices.
c. Contact the cafeteria representative to ask about the menus and see if there is an option
    to seal the nuts in a different way to help avoid the child from being exposed to them.
d. Report the issue to a health official to find out the proper steps to take to ensure that
    the child does not have an allergic reaction in school that could lead to legal threats.

This is the kind of question that has several concerns going on at once: the parent
threatening legal action, whether the cafeteria does a good job of notifying students of
foods that either may contain nuts or are cooked with nut butters, the risk of student
attendance decreasing over a menu item, and bringing additional attention from health
officials over the lunch menu.

The first choice is problematic for schools that have a stricter policy on allowable
material. If needles are not allowed on a school campus, then a policy update may
need to come into play to ensure that EpiPens are an exception to the rule on sharps.
This could raise a larger issue for diabetic students who may have been banned from
carrying around sharps for insulin injections.

The best answer for this question is D. Choice B could significantly affect the
child's grades in the long run. While a school nurse may be equipped to use an EpiPen,
a child will become a regular there if nothing is done about the menus. While Choice
C would help the child know which items to avoid, Choice D would be the best to
advice on health instructions for children's food allergies.

Choice D is also a reasonable option to show that the school cared enough to try
to find the best solution for this child's health care scare. Whatever the health official's tips are on handling possible food items, this practice should then be sent to the
cafeteria staff to implement *after* a trained health professional has been made aware
of the situation.

Tip 8: Cover up the answers.

Revisiting Tip 1 about answering the easiest questions first, make sure the answers are
legitimately that easy and it's not a case of just trying to fly through the exam. Some
test takers will read half the question blurb, not fully read the question, and then just
punch out answers. While it may sometimes work for the test taker who has become
savvy with sample tests or just knows the information back and forth, there's also the
matter of assuming the test taker can read the mind of the test maker.

Even if the test taker knows the information thoroughly, take the extra time to read
the full question before choosing a response. This is different than negatively worded
questions in that the test taker isn't even bothering to find out whether the answer
should be an option to eliminate or an option that is the most correct. This test taker
is just flat-out not reading either way.

For test takers who have an uncontrollable habit of doing this, it is best to treat
themselves like they're cheating by reading the answers. Cover the answer entirely so

wandering eyes won't try to sneak their way down to the answers. Read the full question. Then, slowly move that hand away from all the possible answers, and choose an option. This way, the test taker knows for sure that each question was answered with all of the information needed before making a selection.

Example:
A teacher wants to meet privately with the principal to discuss the possibility of a raise. Although the teacher currently holds a license to teach in that state, the teacher decided to take his experience one step further by taking the NBCTs. What are the NBCTs?

i.   Evaluate the teacher's performance to decide about whether a raise is warranted.
ii. Have a school official look over the terms of the teacher's contract to see if the teacher is eligible for a raise.
iii. Explain to the teacher that because the NBCTs were not a requirement in order to teach at the school nor even requested as a work expense while taking the education courses, the principal is not obligated to pay for the teacher's additional certification.
iv. NBCT stands for National Board Certified Teachers.

For the quick test taker, questions about teacher salaries and certifications will immediately come to mind. The test taker may try to evaluate all that was learned about teacher training from previous sample books. But the question was simple and had nothing to do with finding a resolution to the discussion between the teacher and the principal.

The correct answer is IV.

Tip 9: Don't change the answer without reason.

The one downside of a test taker checking the answers again if there is time is there's also the opportunity to second guess what are probably correct answers. And if those correct answers are changed to incorrect answers, that will really be a disappointment once the test is over, especially if it makes or breaks whether the test taker passed or failed.

Before changing an answer, really consider why the original answer was chosen. The test taker may find that the answer was careless and change the test response to another option. The test taker may believe that the question originally seemed simple and is now wondering whether it really was the correct answer but stays on the safe side and makes no changes.

In this situation, unless the test taker can find a strong reason, such as carelessness or being blatantly incorrect from rushed answers, to change the response, leave it as is. Instead focus on double-checking questions that were more difficult to begin with.

Tip 10: Set a timer for sample test multiple choice questions.

Every test taker will be different when it comes to test-taking time. Some will breeze through certain questions, while it may be more difficult for others. When taking the initial sample test, it is a good idea to take the test straight through just to see how many answers are correct and incorrect.

After taking the initial sample test, go back through the incorrect results and find out why they're wrong. Trying to complete multiple choice questions the other way (looking up possible research and responses to each one) may get the test taker the correct answers, but on test day, test takers just won't have that kind of time and will still have to take into account the constructed-response questions, too.

Tip 11: Process of elimination: Don't be opposed to the guessing game.

Some questions are going to come down to a stroke of luck. Out of four answers and no clue of which one is correct, there's a 25 percent chance that the answer will be correct if guessed. However, there is a 100 percent change it will be marked wrong altogether if no answer is chosen. While a wrong answer may be as bad as a blank answer, the truth of the matter is that the test taker won't know it's wrong when guessing it.

In William Poundstone's book *Rock Breaks Scissors: A Practical Guide to Outguessing and Outwitting Almost Everybody*, the author took a look at whether test takers should opt for guessing.[1]

Of those results summarized by *Business Insider*, the takeaways were:

- "None of the Above" or "All of the Above" was correct more than half of the time.
- The letter or roman numeral answer choice rarely matches the question before it or after it. So if the test taker is stuck on the answer for number 25, and 24 is A and 26 is C, then the answer for number 25 is more likely B or D.
- Sometimes the right answer requires a bit more explaining. If one particular answer is longer than the rest, chances may be higher that that is the correct one to choose.
- Look for the response that doesn't seem to match a pattern of any of the other possible choices. This is usually the choice that is definitely wrong so it can be pulled out of the bunch of possible correct answers.

Now whether the test taker wants to follow these tips is up to each individual person. All of them may be a bit of a stretch.

If "None of the Above" or "All of the Above" is correct over half the time, that still leaves almost the other half that it's incorrect. By now, aspiring principals have seen enough test results to know that sometimes correct answers match. It is indeed possible to have three A's, B's, C's, or D's in a row.

The fourth tip is a mastermind game with computer logic and not worth the trouble. But the third tip seems to be the one that could be the most accurate, especially if the initial wording of it already seemed correct in the first place. If adjectives and phrases are included in this answer, the test maker put far more thought into this particular response than the rest. Make sure no other options are also this long and descriptive before leaning toward lengthy responses.

If guessing which guessing game tactic to use becomes overwhelming, just pick one and remember that there is 25 percent chance of being correct. But guess answers only after all of the other tips have not worked.

Section 7

How to Approach the Essay or Constructed-Response Questions

For the natural writer, being able to answer essay questions or constructed-response questions is the highlight of the exam. This is an opportunity to comprehend, analyze, explain, and summarize what the question is about.

Tip 1: Understand what the test scorer will be looking for in the answer.

While all four are important to answering the question, it is the comprehension part that matters the most. No matter how colorful a written answer may be, if it doesn't effectively explain a problem and potential resolution, it will not help to pass the exam. In both the exams at the end of this book, test takers should be taking notes inside of the book or on sticky notes in order to set up a system of important points to keep in mind.

Example: A fifth-grade student has failed a reading course that required library resources to complete. The parent of the student arrives at the school, complaining that the student was informed that the library resources are ranked for eighth-graders. The school librarians do not deny that the resources are indeed intended for eighth-graders but explains that other students in the course have been able to improve their reading, comprehension, and writing levels from this course. The teacher is unaware that the librarian was using upper-level material.

Should this score stand as is or be removed from the student's record?

Take notes about questions the principal must raise.

1. Who approved the eighth-grade-level material for fifth-graders?
2. Why doesn't the teacher know about what the librarian is using?
3. Did the librarian and teacher work together or separately to create this lesson plan?
4. How was the final grade confirmed if the teacher and librarian did not collaborate together? Was it the teacher's score or the librarians?
5. How did the other students manage to pass the course with better grades than this student? What did they do differently?
6. Are eighth-graders able to use this same material to pass a similar reading course?

Know what the question is asking.

While all of these questions above are imperative for the principal to understand all of the parties involved in using the material, the question is whether the grade should stand. The speedy test taker may spend a great deal of time talking about what to tell the parent, the teacher, and the librarian without ever answering the final question: Is this grade permanent?

Brainstorm on resolutions for each task.

1. Who approved the eighth-grade-level material for fifth-graders?
   a. Review the material to see why it is geared toward eighth-graders instead of fifth-graders.
   b. Make sure the material is not so advanced that it would indeed hinder more than the initial student's grade, too.
   c. Speak with the librarian to find out why this material was chosen as opposed to fifth-grade-level reading material.
   d. Review fifth-grade-level reading material to see if it would be sufficient instead for the child to retake the assigned lessons.
2. Why doesn't the teacher know about what the librarian is using?
   a. Talk to the teacher about familiarity with the project and communication with the librarian.
   b. Inquire about how much the teacher knew about this library project before the students were assigned to complete it.
   c. Inquire about how much the teacher knew about this library project during and after the students were assigned to complete it.
   d. Inquire about whether the teacher had any say in the final grade for the library assignment or were those particular grades just given to the teacher as is.
3. Did the librarian and teacher work together or separately to create this lesson plan?
   a. Find out how the grading scale was used to connect this library project with the teacher's own reading and comprehension lesson plan.
   b. Research whether the two grades should have been separated or combined.
4. How was the final grade confirmed if the teacher and librarian did not collaborate together? Was it the teacher's score or the librarians?
   a. Talk to both the librarian and the teacher to find out why the two didn't work together to collaborate on the grade, if that is the case.
   b. Inquire about which score ranked higher.
   c. Find out how long the library assignment went on and if it should be a certain percentage of the grade.
5. How did the other students manage to pass the course with better grades than this student? What did they do differently?
   a. Compare the library lesson plan results of that student with that of the rest of the class. See what they did different.
   b. Ask the librarian and teacher to also review what this particular student did that led to a failing grade versus other students.
   c. Discuss with the librarian and teacher possible ways that could've helped this student achieve the same test score as the rest.

6. Are eighth-graders able to use this same material to pass a similar reading course?
   a. Look at both passing and failing grades for other eighth-grade students who have also used this material.
   b. Compare what the eighth-grade students did to fail the library lesson plan with what the fifth-grader did to see if there is any correlation.
   c. Ask the librarian and teacher to see if there is any study material that would have helped the failing students along the way for both grades.
   d. Evaluate whether this lesson plan should continue to be used for either eighth-grade or fifth-grade.

Sample answer: While reviewing the scores of eighth-graders who failed the lesson plan and those who passed the lesson plan, there was one major distinction between the two. The students who successfully passed the lesson plan course were also more likely to be better organized across the board when it comes to utilizing systems requiring material in alphabetical order and numerical order, understanding card catalog numbers, identifying library sections, being able to use the online library system to look for material, correctly identifying each book that was asked for in the lesson plan, and knowing what number on the list each student was.

Students who did not do well on the test oftentimes were unable to successfully record the correct names or catalog numbers, identify numerals related to the titles, or choose the correct options online to identify each title.

These organizational differences lead the teacher, librarian, and principal to believe that some students may need to revisit reading and math courses to help with better organization and reading comprehension overall. If the student exhibits general behavior of needing these skills to improve, this grade may be deemed necessary, but the student should be given needed tutoring and lesson practice activities to improve in these areas.

This option should also be made available to eighth-graders experiencing similar learning habits.

While many essay tests grade on the usual formatting of introduction, body, and conclusion, the SLLA test does not. As long as the responses are in a neat format and clearly state how the test taker came to the final conclusion, that is what is scored. It can be a bulleted list, an essay-style format, or a checklist. But the final response must answer the actual question in order to get a perfect score of 3.

Without answering the question, the test taker will more than likely fall into the 1- or 2- level scoring.

Tip 2: Get familiar with key terms and policies.

It doesn't matter if it's pricing, policies, names, dates, or a sequential group of events. It just needs to be a way to keep all key terms in mind before creating a response to the question.

Going back to the question about the library lesson plan, there may be certain educational policies put in place beforehand to explain why this library lesson plan was ranked for a certain grade level. When answering the essay question, being able to identify those policies will either make the lesson plan a valuable asset to the classroom or deem it inappropriate altogether to be immediately removed.

Tip 3: Utilize all material presented for each question.

The scoring system is on a 1–3 scale. Each test taker will have 100 minutes to answer seven separate essay questions. Each question will revolve around a different scenario, and the questions will include additional documentation to help respond to the questions.

This additional material could be letters, newspaper editorials, handouts, tables, graphs, or upper-level policy material. Use all materials to help answer the question correctly. Do not skip over any included material and try to answer the question without it. There will be information within that source that may sway the correct way to answer that particular question.

Tip 4: Know the seven categories to focus on when writing responses.

Each question will be broken down into seven categories.

- Implementation of Vision and Goals
- Data Planning
- Building a Professional Culture
- Curriculum and Instruction
- Assessment and Accountability
- Advocacy—Internal
- Advocacy—External

Tip 5: Know how the test scorer will look at each response individually.

Refer to "How the SLLA Is scored" for more detailed information on this.

The goal of the essay responses is to have a thorough understanding of each question with a focus on one of the seven categories. All responses from test scorers will be divided into thorough understanding, basic or general understanding, limited understanding, or little or no understanding of what the question is asking for.

For example, questions about Visions and Goals may focus on how a new principal would find ways to develop responsibilities for all staff to reach a shared goal. This may also include explaining these new goals to parents, other school staff, students, the media, and more.

Tip 6: Be honest about unclear answers.

Reread the responses to make sure that they make sense to the test taker. If the test taker is confused by his or her own notes or doesn't feel confident in explaining certain policies, procedures, or the conclusion that came from these factors, imagine how perplexed the text scorer will be.

Trying to clean up those same points may require just starting from scratch to reach a new resolution, changing the direction of the questions that the test taker originally wrote out, brainstorming on what that particular policy or resource really means, or being able to clearly explain the test takers' ideas and reasoning.

Tip 7: Provide answers in a logical, sequential pattern.

Revisiting the librarian question, here is an example of a way to respond to that question incorrectly.

Sample answer: Speak with the parent about being unfamiliar with the library lesson plan. Offer steps to eliminate the final grade from the student's record after finding out that the test was eighth-grade-level work. Give the student an alternate assignment to pass the course.

Several reasons why these steps are not effective are:

1. They do not address the larger issue about why this student did not pass the same higher-level test that other students took. Considering some students passed the lesson plan while this student did not, there must be distinct reasons why that should be explored instead of dismissed.
2. If the principal did the footwork to find out that the test is an eighth-grade-level assignment plan, then the communication shouldn't stop there. A conversation with how the teacher and librarian decided to combine these grades (or use one of their grades) should be explored to establish better workplace relationships for them both. These communication skills could also be effective during teacher evaluation time.
3. While honesty is the best policy when speaking with parents, the parent will just grow increasingly concerned about bad communication between the teacher, the librarian, and the principal if the lesson plan was met with a collective shrug by all. It could possibly risk the parent wondering, "What else does this principal not know about? Or the teacher? Should I question other grades, too?"
4. If the reasons that the student did not pass the lesson plan have more to do with reading and math comprehension, the results may be the same with an alternate lesson plan even for a fifth-grade level. Faculty members should explore what went wrong, specifically because a majority of the class was able to pass this same higher-level lesson plan, instead of finding an easier assignment to do just so the student can pass the class.

Tip 8: Do not provide an answer that challenges the question.

Each question and answer on the SLLA exam was already tested and approved beforehand by the test scorer and the consulting supervisor who the test scorers would go to should the scores be too different. While some questions may be more difficult to answer than others, keep the results in mind. Even if the intended results in the question are not what the test taker initially agrees with, stick to the topic at hand.

Going off course and either rewording the question or answering in a way that makes the test taker seem to either not know or not care about the question will immediately result in a lower score. The purpose of the SLLA exam is to be able to take the scenarios in the test seriously, not to edit the questions.

Also, try to stay on the topic of the original question and answer. While personal anecdotes and clever quips may be appreciated in other types of writing, test scorers are looking to make sure the test taker thoroughly understands each question, can recognize what the problem is from the question asked, can create logical steps to figure out results for that question, and get a rationale conclusion.

If the test taker spins off into criticizing the way the classroom is run (e.g., imagine the test taker starts writing about why the card catalog is outdated or not useful in today's school system) or reaching for rationales that were not explored (e.g., how much more difficult it is to find a book using numerical codes versus alphabetical codes), this could lower the score.

Test scorers should also keep in mind that just because something may not be immediately agreeable with their experiences, there are other teachers and principals who collaborated by survey to create these questions and answers. The questions may seem curious because the test taker has not gone through a similar experience, not necessarily a "correct" experience.

Tip 9: Stay away from legalese.

While the test taker may be familiar with an acronym or a buzz word, it is best to treat those responses the way newspapers treat their readers. Don't assume the reader knows what the test taker is talking about on constructed-response questions.

Skip the buzz words, and use common terminology to make the same point. If acronyms and abbreviations must be used, especially if those acronyms or abbreviations have more than one meaning outside of education, introduce the topic with the spelled-out version first. And if the term needs to be used repeatedly again, then it's OK to use the acronym or abbreviation going forward.

Section 8

Preparing for the SLLA Review Exam

Effectively preparing for the SLLA exam may be different for each individual user. Here are a few suggested tips for making the process easier.

UTILIZING PRACTICE EXAMS

Test takers may walk away from the exam feeling like they remembered content during the trial run but not on the official exam. This is normal. The American Test Anxieties Association estimates that 16–20 percent of overall students suffer from high test anxiety,[1] while an additional 18 percent suffer from moderately high test anxiety. However, taking part in practice exams may help eliminate some of the initial worry about completing and passing any exam. Take the practice exams at the end of this book several times. It will familiarize you with the question format and the language of the ISLLC Standards.

While a practice exam will not have the same questions as the final exam, this is an opportunity for students to become more familiar with the material. Is the test taker more savvy at memorizing the general rules for PTA? Is the test taker unsure of just when it is necessary to get health officials involved versus contacting the school custodian? Is the test taker confident in knowing when and how much educational facilities can accept outside gifts, as well as teachers under the principal's guidance?

Taking practice exams is a useful way to get an idea of not only what is on the test but also what a test takers' areas of expertise and weaker areas are. Keep regular notes about which questions are more difficult than others. Keep track of any multiple choice questions and true or false questions that don't seem accurate to the test taker.

If the test taker is puzzled by the answers and thinks they're all "None of the Above," that's a red flag. The same should be said of questions that seem like the answers could be "All of the Above." Remember that the SLLA is unlike other standardized exams. If a question actually does include "All of the Above" or "None of the Above" responses, these may not always be the correct choice. Read the answer choices carefully.

Policies change over time. What may have been a good answer a few years ago may not fit the current educational motto or rules and regulations now. Visit websites and print publications that could help familiarize the test taker with answering these questions not only correctly but in today's current state.

KEEP TRACK OF CHALLENGING ANSWERS ON THE TEST

While memorizing standards, laws, and common policies is important for the SLLA exam, a larger part of the exam involves comprehensive test-taking. Sections of the test include queries on visions and goals, instructing, safety policies, organizational management of educational systems, working with key stakeholders in the educational industry, school goals, interaction with parents and legal guardians, teaching and learning, office management, and the vision for future goals within the departments. Keep track of which standard you are getting questions wrong in and try to understand what that standard's components are. The questions in the practice tests are all aligned to an ISLLC Standard that is provided for you in the answer section.

Questions about these topics may depend not only on the test taker's own business philosophies about how a school should be managed but also on whether they mirror what the ideal school, board members, and parents also want from the organization. In keeping tabs on what questions are answered incorrectly and correctly on the practice exam, pay special attention to any results that the test taker may not agree with. These will more than likely be the most challenging to remember and/or answer correctly when the final exam is taken.

PERSONALIZE INSTEAD OF MEMORIZE

Every test taker is different. Some are experts at memorizing numbers but not policies. Others are much better at remembering student-teacher policies or principal-to-teacher policies but not the best at state health standards. Whatever the area of weakness is, try doing more research on the actual topic as opposed to trying to memorize the answer.

For example, reading about case studies when a new policy was implemented or what the challenges were before an educational facility changed their way of handling issues within that topic matter personalizes it.

For example, say a teacher consistently grades papers late and a parent complains to the assistant principal or principal. Should the principal immediately reprimand the teacher? Contact the assistant principal to deal with the matter at hand? Complete follow-up research to make sure the parent is indeed accurate with stating that grades are late?

Or even if after finding out that the teacher did not distribute grades in a timely manner, should the principal have a private coaching session with the teacher before taking further disciplinary action?

Regardless of what the test taker's initial instincts are for the correct answer, research how other schools handled issues like this. Talk to staff. Talk to mentors. Internalizing real-life examples of how a principal must act in everyday life can become a sticking point around test-taking time.

GO OUTSIDE OF THE BOX TO GAIN INSIGHT

There will probably be questions on the exam that a test taker is not familiar with. It doesn't mean that the actual question is wrong. As with any job, there's always room to learn, and studying for the SLLA exam is an opportunity to also take advantage of outside sources.

Study partners, networking with teachers and principals, and past teacher's assistant positions and internships are all useful. However, consider what other ways to become savvier in the educational world. Unfamiliar with school policies? Sign up for a liability course. Want to learn more about the legal or administrative end of school safety? Check out risk management books and local speaking events or courses.

BEWARE OF TRICKY ANSWERS

For test takers who memorize answers, this may become a bigger issue than those who study for a test in a more comprehensive manner, looking for main points as opposed to keywords, years, days, or policy names. Some answers on the SLLA may in fact be correct answers but not correct for that question.

If there appears to be more than one correct answer, revisit the question. Is one of the answers a direct response to the question while the other answer seems to be more of a tip for later? Is it obvious that one answer has nothing to do with the question although correct on its own merit? Choose the most likely answer in multiple choice options that is most suitable for that particular question.

FULLY COMPREHEND WHAT THE QUESTION IS

Some questions may give a reader extra information, not so much to distract the test taker but to explain why the answer should be what it should be. Say, for example, the question is about a new principal who wants to implement a team-teaching model for her team. The question may be the most important point from the team-teaching model that a principal should share with the staff.

However, the test taker may be so inundated with remembering past study tips about team-building exercises that any one of those responses gets picked instead of the most important one of all of the tips. Know exactly what the question is asking for instead of choosing any relevant data related to the answer.

TAKE ADVANTAGE OF MATH BOOKS, NEWSPAPER STATISTICS

Preparing for the SLLA exam is a perfect opportunity to take a walk through data information that includes pie charts, bar graphs, means, medians, ranges, years, dates, and so forth. Become savvy with reading random statistics. Pick favorite topics in newspapers, books, online articles, and any other topics at hand. While becoming familiar with tabular material based on educational professionals is always a good idea, the bigger picture here is to become fluent in reading visual data.

On test day, don't become so inundated with reading years, dates, percentages, and so forth that answering the actual question goes to the backburner. This may also be a good time to get another type of numbering system involved: clock timers. See how long it takes to answer basic math questions just from reading charts. Ideally, reading statistical data should continue to improve the more often it is done. Take notes on any statistical data that is slower to find an answer to than others. Focus in on those.

KNOWING WHAT'S ON THE EXAM

The exam will be split into the following sections: Visions and Goals, Teaching and Learning, Organizational Systems and Safety, Collaboration with Stakeholders, Ethics and Integrity, and Education System.[2]

The test taker should try to be as strong as possible in each category. While Ethics and Integrity may be more of a negotiable area of expertise than more rigid areas, such as Organizational Systems and Safety (Human Resources and the welfare of students), the SLLA ideally will help test takers have a comfortable level of understanding for all sections.

While SLLA test takers aren't obligated to be experts on all sections involved, the final scores will be calculated on how well the test taker is able to utilize valuable components in order to give fair responses.

For example, in the Teaching and Learning section of the exam, there may be questions about monitoring student progress, team leadership building, knowing when to implement diverse needs for each student based on that student's own past and current performance, or working on standardized instructional programs.

If the question is about how to work with a teacher who cannot take control of a classroom or one with underperforming students, the responses may vary depending on what is the intended goal or the background of the teacher. One teacher may have already established a reputation of unruly classrooms while the next teacher could have been transferred in and is trying to function in a new cultural environment.

These are the kinds of questions where Visions and Goals may be just as important as Teaching and Learning. Some questions may be more interpersonal activities that reflect on the performance of the teacher. Others will be a team effort between the principal, the teacher, and the students. Be aware that the responsibilities (and answers) may change depending on the circumstances mentioned in each question.

GOING WITH YOUR GUT, OR YOUR NOTES INSTEAD

The SLLA exam is timed for each section. When taking the practice exam, the test taker should also try to set the timer to see how many questions can be answered within an allotted time. While the end goal is to be able to answer all questions correctly or fully before time is up, test takers should also take down notes about which questions slowed them down. These notes are not to be confused with the kind of notes taken during the initial studying process. These should be short notes or guesses of what the answers to difficult questions should be.

Once the test taker completes the questions that are easier to answer, revisit those notes with the guessed answers. On second or third read, do those answers still make sense? While it is generally believed that people should "go with their gut," without the added pressure of trying to get through the rest of the test, this is an opportunity for a test taker to reevaluate the question and see if the initial gut reaction answer still makes sense. If it does not, evaluate the rest.

Proceed forward with all missed questions in the same manner until the test is complete or the alarm goes off, notifying the test taker that it's time to put the assignment down. Afterward, when reviewing the sample answers, compare what the original guessed answer was to the questions that were stumbled over. Was that gut instinct correct? Or was the new answer a better choice? Keep those instincts in mind when taking the final SLLA exam.

BE AWARE OF BEST TEST-TAKING PREP LOCATIONS

Anyone who has lived in a college dorm or had a roommate knows that study habits can make or break a living arrangement. The same goes for test preparation. Do not feel confined to study with a partner just because both people are taking the same test if studying habits are drastically different. One person may require music, television, and a revolving door of guests to take "breaks" while reviewing study-guide material. Another test taker would be more comfortable in the furthest aisle of a quiet library with absolutely no foot traffic. Be firm with those choices because there is only one person taking each individual exam, not a group project.

No matter how a student may train for the exam, chances are high that the final exam will be taken in a quieter environment. For the student who has a more challenging time being able to focus and respond to queries without noise around him or her, once the student has mastered the material, it would be useful to take two versions of the exam: one with noise around and one without. Compare the results.

If the results of the practice exams are similar, then there's less to worry about. If the results are different, then it may be time for that student to come outside of the noisy comfort zone and try the exam again. The environment of where the test will be taken will not change; however, the test taker will have plenty of opportunities to alter the answers to correct responses in a change of venue before test-taking day.

CHAT IT OUT WITH OTHER SLLA TEST TAKERS

Even if studying partners must part ways, it doesn't hurt to have team-building days where test takers get together and talk about whatever challenges they're going through with taking the exam. Reverting to the section on "Be Aware of Best Test-taking Prep Locations," this may be a useful opportunity for a test taker to find a better study partner as opposed to a family member, friend, roommate, or another obvious choice that the test taker is regularly around.

Having a mentor or someone who can bond with the SLLA test taker is an opportunity to not only make the studying process a more positive experience but possibly build lasting friendships. In any industry, having a strong support system and valuable business connections can help later on down the line once the exam is complete.

Do not get so burnt out on studying for the exam that by the day of the actual exam, the mind goes blank. Enjoy the company of other test takers (or others outside of that social circle) and reward oneself for a job well done each day.

Become familiar with the 2015 Professional Standards for Educational Leaders, formerly known as the ISLLC Standards.

The standards within the previous ISLLC[3] are "foundational principles of education leadership, which cut across grade levels and help improve student achievement and engagement." Many states across the board utilized these standards in their organizations, which have now transitioned from six standards in 2008 to the 10 below as of November 2015.

The standards used in these tests are an analysis of professional and personal judgment from countrywide industry leaders. Just as the SLLA Review Exam gives a better understanding of how aspiring principals, school superintendents, and other industry leaders would hypothetically react to day-to-day classroom activities, the larger exam also gives test takers a better idea of what people in their industry are already doing in current classrooms.

As with the 2008 version now transitioning into the 2015 updates,[4] the results from these two exams are used to continue to improve on countrywide school systems for the benefit of educational leaders, students, and parents.

Standard 1. Mission, Vision, and Core Values

Effective educational leaders develop, advocate, and enact a shared mission, vision, and core values of high-quality education and academic success and well-being of each student.

Standard 2. Ethics and Professional Norms

Effective educational leaders act ethically and according to professional norms to promote each student's academic success and well-being.

Standard 3. Equity and Cultural Responsiveness

Effective educational leaders strive for equity of educational opportunity and culturally responsive practices to promote each student's academic success and well-being.

Standard 4. Curriculum, Instruction, and Assessment

Effective educational leaders develop and support intellectually rigorous and coherent systems of curriculum, instruction, and assessment to promote each student's academic success and well-being.

Standard 5. Community of Care and Support for Students

Effective educational leaders cultivate an inclusive, caring, and supportive school community that promotes the academic success and well-being of each student.

Standard 6. Professional Capacity of School Personnel

Effective educational leaders develop the professional capacity and practice of school personnel to promote each student's academic success and well-being.

Standard 7. Professional Community for Teachers and Staff

Effective educational leaders foster a professional community of teachers and other professional staff to promote each student's academic success and well-being.

Standard 8. Meaningful Engagement of Families and Community

Effective educational leaders engage families and the community in meaningful, reciprocal, and mutually beneficial ways to promote each student's academic success and well-being.

Standard 9. Operations and Management

Effective educational leaders manage school operations and resources to promote each student's academic success and well-being.

Standard 10. School Improvement

Effective educational leaders act as agents of continuous improvement to promote each student's academic success and well-being.

Section 9

Using Time Effectively

Two of the most common problems with test-taking is spending more time worried about how much time is left on the clock and spending far too much time on one particular answer. No matter whether the question is multiple choice or an essay response, do not spend more than a couple of minutes analyzing it.

Tip 1: Skip the hard questions for later.

If the answers do not immediately come to the test taker, that is OK. Skip it and move on to the next round. Even if it's a question that the test taker is sure was similar to something in the practice exam or a topic that the test taker knew like the back of his or her hand before the timer started, what matters is what's currently going on with the exam.

Anxiety will build up trying to remember one question. That can easily defeat the test taker and make him or her feel less confident in the rest of the exam. Or the test taker could actually "remember" the answer to that question but find himself or herself completely behind in answering the rest of the exam.

Go through the easiest questions first, marking the harder ones, and then revisit the harder ones after the exam is "complete."

Tip 2: Time responses to multiple choice questions versus essay questions.

Unlike multiple choice questions that are a matter of clicking on the correct option, essay questions require just as much concentration, if not more. For the essay portion of the exam, keep in mind that there's the matter of subject-verb agreement, misspellings, tense, clarity, capitalization, and other minute things that make for good or bad writing.

Test takers who love to write may do a better job on the constructed-response questions than on the multiple choice questions. However, skipping past one section to get to the other is not an option on the computerized exam, so the test taker must be prepared to fill in each section before moving on (although skipping multiple choice questions is an option).

When completing the sample exams, the test taker may want to get into the habit of timing himself or herself to see which areas take longer to respond to. Even the most natural writer may find constructed-response questions to take longer than expected. Get more comfortable answering multiple choice questions and constructed-response questions not just factually but in an allotted amount of time.

Tip 3: Take a restroom break if needed even if not wanted.

During the preparation part of the exam, when test takers have more opportunities to get up at their leisure, take a short break to look away from the screen. This gives the eyes, legs, and fingers a chance to relax before diving back in for more information.

On the day of the exam, that 15-minute break won't be possible. But the test taker can still give their eyes a break while preparing for the exam.

In one study,[1] taking a break every 50 minutes of brain-intensive work was connected to higher mental stamina. Human beings are estimated to have an eight-second attention span, one second shorter than a goldfish (nine seconds).

So imagine how easy it is to zone out when a question becomes too difficult, not always from lack of interest but just not being able to focus on it anymore or being too overwhelmed with other parts of the exam.

If there is an option for a bathroom break during the exam, without hurting the allotted time to complete the exam, take it. Even test takers who are on a roll and feel like they don't need a break make benefit from stretching their legs, using the facilities and getting a beverage.

Tip 4: Give the eyes a chance to breathe.

This is also an excellent opportunity to give the eyes some rest for computerized exams. Eyestrain, headaches, blurred vision, dry eyes, and neck pain are all linked to staring at a computer screen for too long.[2]

Poor seating posture and the glare from a computer screen are also linked to computer vision syndrome. Now imagine how much time has already been used staring at a computer screen during the research, completing practice exams, and speaking with other test takers about the exam. That's a lot of strain on the eyes.

Optometrists suggest looking away from computer screens into the distance for 20 seconds after every 20 minutes of computer use.

Tip 5: Consider a speed-reading course.

The average speed of reading for a fifth-grader is 173 words per minute. The average speed of reading for the average person is 250 words per minute. However, speed readers can read as fast as 650 words per minute. However, that doesn't mean the information is always retained.

During the studying process, try this speed-reading test from the *Wall Street Journal*[3] to calculate how much the test taker can read a short article. Then answer a few questions. Then take one of the three speed-reading tips to find out first how much faster one can read with speed-reading tips. Measure that by how many answers are correct during the speed-reading process.

Try all three tips: Avoid the inner voice reading in the test taker's head. Guide fingers or a computer mouse pointer to read along or peripheral vision. Keep in mind that the peripheral vision tip is an expert-level option that may take more time to practice.

Some test takers may find that although they are reading faster, they're also getting more answers incorrect. For other test takers, it may be the opposite.

While it certainly couldn't hurt to find out a few tips to be able to get through a test faster, if like this online speed-reading test all of the answers are incorrect, it may not do everyone the same amount of good. But for others, it could make getting through dense material much easier.

Tip 6: Avoid burnout before the exam.

This can happen to even the best test taker. The test taker burns the midnight oil, learns policies, and becomes familiar with all seven themes. And the day of the test, somehow this same test taker just cannot focus on writing or understanding the test. It's not that the information on the test is strange territory. Sometimes test takers can just be burned out.

Frequent reasons for burnout[4] include:

* Long-term fatigue from studying
* Intellectual exhaustion
* The brain shutting down on trying to absorb more information
* Refusing to study further or learn new material
* Academic performance lowering or poor results from the sample exam
* Indifference toward educational topics

Even while studying for the exam, test takers should know when they've reached the burnout arena. Surefire signs of burnout include hunger, irritation, answering questions incorrectly that the test taker knows they're familiar with, daydreaming, or not being able to understand simple instructions.

While all of these burnout habits are easy to recognize, the last one in particular can be tricky. A test taker who is trying to cram more information in may think the information is more difficult than it really is. Or, the test taker may read lines of text, forget what was read, and have to read the same text over and over again.

If this happens while studying for the exam, get up immediately and take a break. It will be a disservice in the long run to not be able to retain useful information for the final exam. If this happens during the exam, skip to another question or take a break, even if it's as simple as referring to the computer vision syndrome tricks.

Tip 7: Approach studying to learn rather than to pass the test.

One of the most useful parts about the SLLA exam is the test is geared toward on-the-job knowledge and past experiences as opposed to memorizing terms and tips. That doesn't mean that there won't be certain guidelines that a principal must follow in order to be effective at the job.

The data section of the exam provides resources that the principal must follow in order to utilize a school's educational guidelines. But there's a reason that sites like

PsychCentral[5] suggest focusing on learning as opposed to the grades, and this mindset will help test takers on the exam.

In theory, any time an exam is based on experience and a test taker can personalize the test questions and answers, this will help them think constructively about the questions. Grad school students should have already figured this tip out, comparing their undergraduate work to upper-level master's programs, internships, and teaching assistant opportunities.

During the studying process, if the test taker uses the test to learn from the tips and answers, these lessons will be retained long after the exam is over. Hopefully, the test taker will be able to relate to some or all of the questions along the way, assuming they've had the opportunity to experience these concerns in their educational background. And if the test taker cannot relate to a question personally, consider previous mentors and other workplace professionals who have had to work on similar issues.

Tip 8: Be able to identify when test notes aren't helpful.

Consider the best ways to retain and utilize notes throughout the test taker's career and educational opportunities. There is no hard and fast rule for how a test taker should take notes that make sense to them. Just make sure those note-taking tips are actually useful while taking the practice and final exam.

In tips for preparing for the exam, be mindful that outlines are recommended to further explain and explore points that will need to be made for the essay part of the exam. However, there is such a thing as overkill on note-taking. Do not take too many notes, concentrate on completing the exam in a timely fashion. Be brief when notetaking. If the test taker finds himself or herself spending more time trying to make sense of the notes than actually formulating an answer to the question, it might be time to stop. Reevaluate what's on the page, and then either rewrite those notes or rework the original theory.

One of the most common ways that test takers end up with lower scores is by going off point. Test takers who may either take too many notes or ineffective notes will almost certainly find themselves transitioning away from the question.

Sample question: The physical education teacher announces to a class of students that she would like to incorporate a nutrition lesson into their grades in order to pass the course. A student tells her parent about this nutrition addition to the physical education course, and the parent complains to the principal.

According to the parent, the student would be better off being physically active than doing more sedentary activities writing down nutritional goals and doing computer-based research on food. The physical education instructor strongly believes that nutrition and fitness work together. How should the principal work with both parties to reach an amicable resolution?

Poor test-taking notes: In this particular scenario, an example of poor note-taking would be if the test taker wrote down a list of possible nutritional guidelines to follow as opposed to reviewing what the physical education teacher has already introduced to the class. The test taker would be adding on more unnecessary work without first reviewing what could already be a quality program.

Better test-taking notes: One of the first steps should be to review the actual program that the physical education teacher already introduced to the students. If this program could be useful to students, better notes would be how to present this plan to the parent. Suggestions may include confirming with a health expert why both nutrition and physical fitness matter at an early age as opposed to one or the other. Or, maybe exploring the idea of making the nutritional lesson plan homework so the student will continue to participate in physical activity, as the parent requested.

Tip 9: Sequential order second, comprehension should be first.

On the same topic of note-taking, it may seem counterintuitive to tell a test taker to write the first topics that come to mind instead of writing in sequential order. There will be the opportunity to fix those steps on the final answer.

However, when a test taker is trying to figure out all of the steps that must be followed in order to complete a task, jotting down whatever comes to mind first or any important points helps. The test taker can always change the order of them once each task or step is spread out.

Sample answers for nutrition and fitness question:

1. Review the nutrition tips to make sure they are relevant for the student's age group.
2. Speak with physical education teacher to inquire about why this particular nutrition lesson plan was chosen.
3. Inquire with the physical education teacher how much time would be dedicated to the physical fitness portion of the class versus the nutrition portion of the class.
4. Ask the parent how much flexibility would there be if the nutrition course took up less time than the physical fitness part of the class (e.g., 75 percent versus 25 percent).
5. Research how effective programs like this have been for other students, preferably in the local school system.
6. Find out whether the student was already doing a good job of participating in physical activity. If the student enjoys physical activity more in this course, this is a good opportunity to get the student involved.

Discuss with the physical education teacher why the course would be better by incorporating nutrition lesson plans, specifically if the course previously focused only on making sure students were active for a required amount of time in the day.

Inquire with the parent about ways that would lead to a change of heart for the nutritional program. For example, if students are encouraged to work together on an active field trip to a grocery store or take part in a gardening project, these are two ways for students to be active and at the same time learn about nutrition.

For this particular question, all of the variables will be needed before making a final decision between both the teacher and the parent. If the principal knows more about the program and can either explain its merit to the parent or have the teacher do so, this problem may easily be resolved.

If the test taker wants to go back to those answers and change the order of them later, that is OK. But the test scorer is looking for logical responses that clearly explain how to resolve the question. Don't spend unnecessary time on things the test scorer will not grade the test taker on.

However, there may be parts of the exam where sequential order will matter more, such as Managing Organizational Systems and Security versus Collaborating with Key Stakeholders.

Tip 10: Recognize when answers should require more time explaining about how to work as a team versus working individually.

This may be one of the biggest obstacles for a natural born leader, especially in the world of business and/or education. The section on Collaborating with Stakeholders focuses on working within teams. Out of all of the sections, this one may be most important to note that test takers should approach each question with themes about teamwork and participation.

On top of answering a question correctly, the test scorer will take note of whether the test taker knows when to reel in a list of orders and when to ask stakeholders for assistance. If the sample question above was in the category for stakeholders, it would be especially important to consider getting students, teachers, and parents involved before making a final decision on the nutrition course.

Tip 11: Don't be afraid to introduce new ideas.

This is a useful opportunity not only for the principal to establish great communication skills and an open-door policy with the teacher but also to make the parent feel like his or her opinion matters for what is being taught in the school.

Students may often feel like they're seen but not heard, so incorporating how the student of the concerned parent plus the rest of the students feel about the course could do more to help with additional physical education courses down the line.

In some schools, this particular onetime course could be more useful as its own standalone course if other stakeholders are willing to get onboard. The teacher in the sample question doesn't have to be the only person to decide to suggest something innovative for teachers and students. The test taker can be, too, but any new ideas must be effectively explained while staying on the topic of the end result: bringing the parent onboard for the new course or getting rid of the idea altogether.

Section 10

Effective Tips and Approaches

Being in any leadership position means being able not only to dictate orders and be confident in a well-researched position but also to work well with stakeholders. For principals, those stakeholders include auxiliary personnel (janitors, cafeteria workers, bus drivers); affiliated businesses and churches; teachers; librarians; counselors; and parents.

Tip 1: Keep a holistic approach in mind before and after the exam.

While the teacher is concentrating on grades, the cafeteria workers will examine nutrition. While the librarian is paying attention to outdated and incoming supplies for better learning, the bus driver is all about time management. While the parent is concerned about a child's grades, the child may be as focused on the grades as he or she is in a social life.

Principals have to take on the holistic approach to it all: culture, attitude, atmosphere, instruction, curriculum, student and teacher development, social circles, laws, and day-to-day operations. But there is also the matter of finances and business management that some stakeholders may not have the same inside scoop on.

Financial woes, fundraising, personnel hiring and termination, budgeting, safety, and facility costs must also factor into the decisions that a principal makes. This is one of the many reasons that the multiple choice questions and constructed-response questions take on so many issues. Principals must be able to fluently move from one set of educational structures and goals to another.

Tip 2: Being optimistic doesn't mean not being realistic.

While taking the SLLA exam, aspiring principals should approach the questions from an idealistic perspective but still keep in account realistic results. There may be answers on the test that seem like they could be a good idea, but test takers can quickly become skeptical of whether that solution would actually work. Pick the best choice for a school instead of choosing strategies that may be more common.

As with any business, there is always room for growth and change is not out of the question. As long as the responses are moral and useful and help to make a facility run smoothly, those are the answers that should count most of all.

Tip 3: Do not obsess over the perfect score.

Questions are rated on a scale of 1–3, with 3 being the best answer. While it is important to understand the feedback for the most high-ranking scores and lowest scores, do not become more distracted by the scoring number than answering the question. An ideal test would have all scores rated as 3, but it is counterproductive to assume that a score of 2 did not have good information.

If the feedback from each answer is available, take those notes and scores as ways to improve upon the results later on in the test taker's career field. Also, keep in mind that during the testing process, different test scorers will be reading the answers. If their scores for one constructed-response answer are too different, an additional test scorer will be assigned to read the same question and answer to make the final thought.

This process alone should help put the test taker at ease that what may be a superb answer to one person could be average to another. Even the test scorers must pass a test before being given their positions. And their scores are continuously reviewed to ensure honest scoring, in addition to new test scorers being introduced to the team each testing season. This may not only be helpful for veteran test scorers but also an opportunity for new test takers to have their scores looked at by fresh eyes.

Tip 4: The test taker has the right to utilize all four hours.

If, for some reason, the test must start later than expected, the test taker will still be given the opportunity to use the entire time[1] no matter what the official starting time was. However, the supervisors at the testing center will make every effort to start the test at its scheduled time.

Of course, no one can predict what will happen on the test day, but test supervisors are cognizant of health-related causes and any other reasonable incident that may cause a delay.

However, the test taker should also put in as much due diligence to avoid anything that could possibly decrease the timeframe for testing. That includes making sure online admission forms are filled out, proper and valid identification are brought to the testing center, restricted items are left at home or in a secure location, all health-related topics are discussed weeks beforehand that may require extended periods of testing, and there is sufficient time management for each question and answer.

Tip 5: Don't be afraid to think outside of the box.

Piggy backing on Tip 2, test takers should also keep this time in mind while working on the constructed-response questions. Provide honest, useful feedback for how to resolve the incidents described in each question. The test taker should keep his or her own professional experiences in mind while responding to each question, in addition to what has worked well in the past.

Do not approach the test the way a job interviewee would approach a cover letter for an entry-level job interview. The cover letter for a job interview is used to introduce strangers to job recruiters who have no idea if this person has the qualifications to complete the job. The resume is supposed to provide proof of what the cover letter may not have covered. However, the SLLA exam is designed for people who already have experience in the educational field and can approach their answers as a qualified leader as opposed to the entry level.

The test taker should utilize the skills that he or she has already acquired to respond to constructed-response questions, as well as multiple choice questions, as opposed to filling in what that person guesses will be the correct answer or the correct response.

Should the SLLA test taker pass the exam and be licensed to work in a particular state, stakeholders will count on that same honesty in the exam to be used on a daily basis in the school. Think of the test as an internal hiring position. The industry already knows the test taker. The test is just designed to make sure that all of these skills and experience can sufficiently transfer over to a new organization.

Tip 6: Try to avoid careless mistakes.

The day of the exam can be a lot of pressure, especially for test takers who know for sure that they have studied hard and were confident after taking the sample exam. Do not let nerves get in the way of taking the exam and possibly risk making careless mistakes.

Those careless mistakes can include:

- Not filling in the correct identification on the first page, including Social Security number and correct mailing address.
- Skipping over multiple choice questions and not going back to fill them in. Even if the answer is a guess, there's the possibility that that answer may be correct. Leaving a multiple choice question blank leaves 100 percent chance to get it wrong altogether.
- Not paying attention to or purposely skipping over the computer instructions for how to get back to those same skipped questions.
- Not reading the entire question in the constructed-response sections. This could lead too easily to answering a question that wasn't asked or repeating what is already in the question.
- Not answering the actual question that is asked. Anyone who has ever pulled out their smartphones or notebooks to create a To Do list and forgot what should be on it will relate to this. Sometimes test takers can spend so much time preparing to answer a question or jotting down off-topic notes and totally forget that they never completed the most important part.
- Not proofreading the answers to avoid unnecessary typos, misspellings, incorrect punctuation. Although five-part essay answers aren't required to complete the constructed-response questions, the written approach should still be neat and as easy as possible for the test scorer to comprehend.
- Not taking suggested breaks. Even if the test taker is on a role, there will be a point where the eyes, the legs, the head, and even the fingers will get tired of typing and

focusing on a computer screen. Take the time to give the eyes a break and the body a chance to recoup for Round 2 or Round 3 of the test-taking process. The scores won't be any higher just because the test taker chose to ignore restroom breaks.

Tip 7: Know who to study with.

Tips for finding the correct study partner are covered in the "Preparing for the SLLA Review Exam" part of this booklet, but are worth noting again. Test takers should work with other SLLA test takers who have like minds.

These are people who will have effective time management skills and allow the test taker to sufficiently read and review any unfamiliar questions or answers. Study partners should also be helpful in suggesting and helping to remember useful test-taking tips.

Find a study buddy online.
For SLLA test takers who may not have someone local to help them prepare for the exam, don't give up. Consider finding an online study buddy. Websites like MoocLab[2] let test takers register online and search for others.

Or, consider trying to find other study buddies on social media. One quick hashtag and keyword search on social media website Twitter[3] brought up plenty of people who either already took the exam or are studying for it now. This is an opportunity to speak to others about what useful tips they took in order to pass the exam.

Discuss past school experiences through networking.
There's a large possibility that most of the constructed-response questions won't be topics that the test taker has direct experience with, but chances are higher that these are topics that have happened to other current principals or current teachers. Ask around. Go to academic networking events.

Consider creating a MeetUp[4] to talk with other teachers, and discuss what their personal experiences were with handling various issues. Sometimes their advice about what worked and didn't work at the school they currently work for, intern with, or are completing a teaching assistant position for could help come exam time.

Consider letting each study partner complete an outline to share.
Test takers should play to their strengths. If one is better at teamwork sections and another is good at policy note-taking, choose those sections as the ones to focus on. Then, group partners can share their notes with the other later. Sharing study notes for a test that neither party has taken is still honest, and it's also an opportunity to be able to look at the sample questions and answers in a different way. The study partner may also have an easier way of explaining the lesson plan than the test taker taking notes alone.

Tip 8: Look for the wrong answer, not the right answer.

With EXCEPT, NOT, and LEAST questions, choosing the incorrect answer is the obvious technique. However, this may also come in handy for completing multiple choice questions and constructed-response questions.

For multiple choice questions that are more difficult, review all of the answers and look for the ones that are obviously wrong. Mark a symbol (e.g., asterisk *) next to those, so if that question is skipped over, the test taker knows what remaining answers to choose from.

For TRUE and FALSE questions, even if the test taker isn't sure which option to choose, take side notes about anything that could possibly make the question true or not.

Example: The principal has installed a suggestion box at the entrance doorway. While reviewing some of the suggestions, the principal reviewed one student's suggestion to improve the HTML coding courses to include content management systems. However, one of the computer teachers disagreed with this suggestion, pointing out that personal homepage or hypertext preprocessor (PHP) and structured query language (MySQL) courses should be considered instead. Is the computer teacher correct?

a. True
b. False

For the computer savvy test taker, WordPress is one of the most popular sites that may come to mind, and this site is indeed a content management system that uses PHP and MySQL.

Text Box 10.1

Absolutely	Certainly	Nobody
Absolutely not	Certainly not	No one
All	Forever	None
Always	Invariably	Only
Best	Never	

But even if the test taker does not know this, the abbreviations for coding options should set off a mental alarm that either this student has much to learn about web

Text Box 10.2

A few	Many	Much	Some
A majority	May	Often	Sometimes
Apt to	Might	Probably	Unlikely
Frequently	Most	Seldom	Usually

coding or the student knows so much that he or she wants others to be better at it. In this case, the answer is FALSE.

Look for keywords that can be questioned and may be too exaggerated to mark as FALSE.[5] These keywords include:

Also, look for keywords that provide room for exceptions and may be able to debate. These are usually TRUE.

While constructed-response questions aren't as easy to identify with simple right or wrong answers, the test taker can also jot down notes for topics that should be questioned while answering a question.

Using this same sample question, possible notes may be:

If the computer teacher believes that PHP and MySQL should be explored more and the student wants to lean more toward content management systems, can't both topics be incorporated together? TRUE

Is the computer teacher not incorporating content management systems into the regular lesson plan? TRUE (if judging from the suggestion of the student)

Is computer web coding a useful topic in today's tech savvy world? TRUE (Both the computer teacher and the student found the topics relevant enough to speak on them. Neither party mentioned anything about the systems being older or outdated, only that certain elements may not be explored enough when talking about the other.)

Tip 9: Learn about your test center.

If possible, take a trip to your SLLA testing location during the final week before the exam. Learn how to get there so that you don't get lost on exam day. Try and find out what room the exam will be administered in and ask to see the room. This will make sure that you don't encounter any surprises when you sit for the exam (e.g., small desks, cold or hot rooms, clock locations, etc.). If possible, take a timed prep test by yourself at the testing location. Anything that helps you become more comfortable in the testing environment will minimize unwanted stress on the day of the exam.

Tip 10: Ignore everyone else on test day.

This may be one of the toughest parts of taking the test. There have been study groups, meeting sessions, phone discussions, social media networking, plenty of chatting about the test with loved ones, and talking to other like-minded professionals. On test day though, this is not a time to people watch or look at what other people are doing outside of the supervisor at the testing center.

If someone else finishes the exam first, appears to be distracted, or takes multiple breaks during the exam, it is their business. Each test taker works on the final test alone. For that reason alone, work alone.

Part III

PRACTICE EXAMS

Practice Test One

Questions

65 Multiple Choice and 1 Constructed Essay

1. The newly hired principal at Martin Luther King, Jr. High School faced the challenge of starting a new year after a spring of cultural clashes between students had closed the school a week early. Arriving in June he spent long days examining data about the school. The school had a vision statement that was also called the school goal. He found no objectives that would lead the school toward that vision.

   What action should the principal take to start the development of a plan of action to get the school off to a safe, educationally focused, and academically rigorous year?

   (A) Send a letter to all parents telling them that he would have a plan in place for the fall and to conference with their children, letting them know the he would not tolerate any violence.
   (B) Ask the superintendent to develop a police presence in his school full-time.
   (C) Send letters out to teachers, students, and parents inviting them to attend two of three evening sessions that would be held previous to the start of school and for the purpose of the development of a several small community/school groups to work with the school to evaluate their vision, set goals, and objectives to meet those goals.
   (D) Get a plan together and send it to teachers and parents and ask them to attend a meeting at the school on one of two evenings so he could communicate the plan with them.

2. In the second year as principal of Roosevelt Middle School, the district decided that all teachers, specialists, and coaches would take responsibility for a 30-minute period at the end of each day for relationship building, clubs, assemblies, homework help, and school-wide student training that was required. At each grade level, students would be divided randomly into classes for this part of the day. Due to the nature of these sessions, there was a tone of discontent with much of the faculty. Some did not feel comfortable helping with math homework, and coaches often had to leave with teams before the day was over. Special education teachers were worried they did not have enough support at that time of day due to limited para-professionals.

How should this principal proceed?

(A) The principal must hold a faculty meeting, inviting the superintendent, and let them know this is a district-wide change to follow the vision of a more student-centric model and there was really no other option.

(B) The principal held a faculty meeting and impressed upon the faculty that this was a mandate from the district, but he would love for the teachers to develop a group who would commit time to address such concerns and bring a more plausible arrangement. He agreed to support what the teachers felt would work best within the district's vision.

(C) The principal should handpick teachers he knew were easy to work with and got along well together and bring them into his office to try and work this out.

(D) The principal should find out how other schools in his district planned to implement this change and use their plan.

3. During the school year the math teachers decided to move their lower students into one class and the more advance into another. It went against the school's vision and district's stress to have high expectations for all students and to maintain equity and inclusion of all.

   After noticing lots of class schedules being changed, the principal went to the counselor and asked why this was happening. She told him the math teachers had requested the moves.

   Which of the following responses by the principal conforms to the most acceptable leadership practice?

(A) Tell the counselor in no way was she to permit any more schedule changes without her approval.

(B) Call in the math teachers together and question their actions.

(C) At the next staff meeting remind all teachers of the school's vision and that research supports the district's vision to maintain class diversity in all ways.

(D) Call each math teacher into her office and discuss the situation, reminding teachers of the school's mission and help each teacher to write an effective plan to improve teaching strategies to include all students and then monitor that plan.

4. In an interview for a candidate seeking an administration position, the candidate was asked how he would cope with the greatly reduced budgets, the poverty of the families in this school, and increasing class sizes.

   Which reply would demonstrate the candidate's knowledge, professionalism, and strategic thinking ability?

(A) Because I know the mission and vision of the school is to partner with local families in academic success, I would lead that mission by strengthening the bonds between the community and school, to be creative in a search for support, and to focus on the positive aspects of our community and school, building on that pride to give energy to meet our goals.

(B) I would gather the faculty and community together to send every kind of communication to our legislature to change the situation.

(C) I would focus on adding volunteers in the classroom to assist teachers with larger class sizes and begin a campaign to end poverty in our community.

(D) Because I know the school is also struggling academically, I would start an after-school program to help kids with homework and give them a snack.

5. At Ben Franklin Elementary, the grade-level teams were finding it difficult to plan together. Professional collaboration was one of the goals for the school. The teachers have come to you to ask for help with the scheduling to make this happen.

   What will be the key to leading them in reaching this goal?

   (A) Requesting more money to hire subs for them a half day a week.

   (B) Ask if they'd be willing to stay after school an hour once a week so this important opportunity would take place.

   (C) Sit down with the specials teachers, art, music, and physical education, to see if the schedule could be changed so all grade levels went to specials at the same time.

   (D) Get parent volunteers to come in and stay with the classes once a week.

6. You will be opening the new middle school in the district. Your staff will all be newly working together and you will need to spend time at the beginning of the year, during teacher work days, setting a vision with goals for the school. It's going to be difficult with everyone trying to prepare for their classes. You will need an entire day to get through a discussion to accomplish the task. You could use two half days. Because it is so important to begin with a set of high expectations, a child-centered education and student support, your decision on this action will set the tone for the rest of the year.

   Which of the following actions would best demonstrate to his teachers that he understands their time is important, that setting goals and a vision is also very important and he highly values their input.

   (A) He should just decide to spend the first day back at the task and tell the teachers they may have to come in a few days early to complete their classroom planning.

   (B) He should send out a letter to the faculty explaining that he does not want to waste their time, so he's taken it upon himself to write up several vision statements with goals and objectives and they need to e-mail a vote for one.

   (C) He should send out a letter to the faculty asking them for ideas for a vision statement and goals and volunteers to meet on the first day to work these into one statement that could be presented on the second day of staff meeting and save a lot of time.

   (D) He could postpone this action until after school has started.

7. It is your first year as an administrator. The office staff is often heard gossiping about students, families, and teachers. Because they have worked at this school for years, they have lived in the community for years, and they are much older than you are, you are hesitant to mention the problem.

   As the educational leader of the school, you should

(A) Leave them alone. If they've been there for years apparently, it has not been a problem.

(B) Send them all an e-mail stating new office policies and add there will be no gossip. Then sign them up for training about professionalism in the workplace.

(C) Get a teacher who has been there a long time and is friendly with them to talk to them about the ethics of talking about private or personal issues within the school day.

(D) Call them into your office separately and explain that because the office sets the tone of the building, you'd like their help to add some professionalism by keeping talk to office work, keeping talk quieter, and eliminating all personal references to students, teachers, or parents out of conversation.

8. The district is making financial cuts, and that means smaller classes and moving teachers around. Everybody is talking about who will have to move to another school. You've been informed by one teacher that there are rumors about certain teachers having to move schools and some are getting ugly about it.

    What is your position in this state of affairs?

    (A) It is not your affair. It is a district decision and you need to wait until the district makes decisions and then you will deal with it.

    (B) Have a faculty meeting and openly discuss the issues. Tell the teachers when the final word comes down about how many teachers the student numbers will allow your school to keep, you will have a district resource person come and discuss how those decisions will be made.

    (C) Have a faculty meeting and tell the teachers that you've heard there is conflict about this situation that hasn't even happened yet; it has to stop and you will let them know when you know something.

    (D) Ignore the gossip. It's just part of a school culture for teachers to always growl and grumble and fear the worst. If they are good teachers, they will be glad to just have a job.

9. Students at your high school have a rally in front of the school for prayer every Wednesday. There are those who don't like it. They say prayer needs to stay out of the schools. Some parents go by and honk their horns to disrupt it. Others are adamant that it will continue.

    As the administrator, what would be the best way to handle this?

    (A) Send out communication to all parents that this is a right protected by the constitution, and it would demonstrate an appreciation of our rights if they would not honk.

    (B) Tell the kids to go behind the building to have their prayers to prevent the problems.

    (C) Have the history teachers take a day or two to discuss the basis for our rights and personal freedoms and why it is so important. This is an opportunity to learn.

    (D) Have an assembly and let an important government official give a speech about our freedoms.

10. Ford High School reading scores on the state assessments are mediocre. The district developed a series of eight workshops to help teachers at that school effectively teach reading skills. The workshops would begin in August with one each month the first semester and three more spread across the second semester. The teachers were taught specific practices that were meant for their content area and their own classrooms. At the end of the year the district asked the administrator of Ford High to evaluate the effectiveness of the classes.

   Of the following methods for evaluation, which one is appropriate to assess the effectiveness of this series of workshops?

   (A) He prepared a set of tests that covered the entire series and gave it after the final workshop to evaluate what the teachers had learned.
   (B) He asked the teachers to write an evaluation and include what they did in their classrooms differently, which methods they used more often, and their opinion as to whether they felt the workshops were worth the time and cost.
   (C) He pulled the state reading scores of students from last year and compared them with state reading scores in the current year to evaluate the effectiveness of the workshops.
   (D) He had the reading teacher pull random students in to take a basic reading inventory to see if they scored at grade level.

11. A parent reported to a school board member that several of their local high school teachers had been drinking at the local brewery and discussing students quite openly. This parent was appalled at the unprofessional behavior. The information was directed to the principal of the high school for evaluation. After calling the teachers individually into his office, and finding out they did take part in such a conversation, it required a response.

   Which of the following is NOT an appropriate response to this situation?

   (A) Encourage each teacher to call the woman, admit their indiscretions, and apologize for breaking the trust the community should be able to have in teachers at their schools.
   (B) Attend a workshop on ethics and professionalism.
   (C) Explain to the teachers that when they are unethical, it can lead to disruption in the academic focus of the school and trusting relationships with students.
   (D) Because it was the first time it happened, they were told not to do it again or they would be transferred to a different school.

12. Ms. Andrews is the associate principal in a large inner-city school. The mix of cultures of students and teachers is diverse and misunderstandings often result in conflict, tension, and interrupted classwork. She has been asked to develop a series of events to bring about a higher level of understanding and promote an atmosphere where everyone will embrace their differences throughout the next three years. The district wants a change and wants to see that change measured. Of the following, what is the most effective order to accomplish this task?

   (i) Gather a task force of parents, students, teachers, and community leaders.

(ii) Develop some polls, questionnaires, and rating scales to gain insight and set a measureable score for the purpose of comparison in three years.

(iii) Use various stakeholders to form committees to brainstorm productive events or activities.

(iv) Develop a long-range plan for meetings, events, and activities for the three years.

    (A) III, II, I, IV

    (B) II, I, III, IV

    (C) IV, I, III, II

    (D) II, III, I, IV

13. A large group of immigrants from the Middle East settled in the community over the summer. Ms. Andrews, the principal at Jefferson Elementary, wants to start the year off with some specific activities to incorporate the new students, their culture, and their families immediately.

    Wanting to be accurate about their culture and countries but not touch on the tragedies of the war they left behind, Ms. Andrews reviews some ideas with her lead teachers before school begins.

    Which of the following statements describes the most effective first step in the development of activities?

    Hold a family cultural event day on a weekend with fun activities, food, and people from several different cultures for the entire community.

    (A) Invite some of the families to meet with the leadership team just to get to know them. Serve appropriate refreshments and have an interpreter ready.

    (B) Begin school with a unit on the country from which the new residents immigrated and incorporate some of the children or parents to talk about their culture.

    (C) Send out information to all families in your school to join the school in welcoming the newcomers at a back-to-school event to meet and greet each child and family.

14. You are the administrator of a high school in a small district, and during the year there has been movement toward cultural cliques that have become more aggressive each month. In order to reverse this movement, you have developed a committee of teachers who've either shown interest and concern or who you feel might connect with many of these students. This committee has met several times and are ready to present their goals to you and the rest of the staff. They want the entire staff to be part of the goal setting and have total participation in the path the committee takes toward increasing student respect between diverse groups.

    From the following list of long-range goals, which fits best with how you want to lead the school?

    (A) The students will, by the end of the current year, demonstrate a decrease in negative interaction between cultural groups, as reported by student, parent, or staff, by half.

    (B) The students will, by the end of the year, demonstrate an increase in social interaction between cultural groups, as reported in a teacher survey, by 50 percent.

(C) The students will, by the end of the year, demonstrate less negative interaction between cultural groups, as noted in a parent survey, by 50 percent.

(D) The students will, by the end of the year, demonstrate increased positive student interaction between cultural groups, as noted in anecdotal reports taken from adults in charge of social events, by 50 percent.

15. Mr. Maxwell is the administrator of Truman Elementary School. There are eight special needs students in the fourth-grade classes. The teachers have the para take those students to the library during your science class because it is too difficult for them. When you realize this was happening, you check their IEPs and see that the only service for these students in science is a para-professional in the classroom.
    What action should you take?

(A) You take no action since it appears to be working well.

(B) You report this to the resource teacher.

(C) You tell the para-professional that she needs to keep the students in the general classroom.

(D) You talk to the teachers about it and remind them that inclusion in that part of the day is about more than merely learning science, and because the IEP states they are in the classroom, you offer more resources for her support.

16. A student with an IEP that addresses behavioral issues brings a knife to school. You call the parents and ask that they pick him up and keep him at home until the team can decide how to proceed. You immediately set up a meeting with the IEP team and include the district special education coordinator.
    What is this meeting called?

(A) An IEP referral meeting

(B) A manifestation hearing

(C) A detention hearing

(D) A police inquiry

17. In an elementary school that is a mix of lower and upper economic areas, the teachers want to start an after-school program for kids who live in the run-down apartments. They have targeted this population as most in need of help to increase state scores on assessments. If the school does this, they can supply a bus to take them home after the program. The principal tells the teachers he cannot approve this plan.
    Which of the following statements is the basis for his lack of approval?

(A) The school cannot afford to pay for the bus.

(B) First they must find available staff to work in the program.

(C) Students in that area will never stay after school.

(D) Any program developed for students because of where they live or upon the basis of their economic situation is based on biased thinking.

18. You are newly hired as principal of a high school in a small community where there is no racial or cultural diversity. You have been asked to come up with programs that will promote student interaction with people who are more diverse

to prepare them for the world beyond their borders. After meeting with students, staff, and parents, your group decides to collect shoes for an African country in need. (This scenario will be used to answer questions 7 and 8.)

What is wrong with this idea?

(A) It does not support the goal.
(B) The community could never gather enough shoes to be successful.
(C) It requires too much school time to collect and box up shoes to send overseas.
(D) It will take too many athletes out of after-school sports.

19. An administrator in curriculum and instructional resources is to assign new teachers in the district for the purpose of support. She meets with them as a group once a month. In the first meeting two teachers shared their feelings of floundering with classroom management. She is encouraged that they have opened up to the group and feels as though there might be others with some of the same issues.

From this point, what would be the most helpful response for the administrator to take?

(A) Schedule individual conferences to analyze, prioritize, and examine various strategies that could be put into place.
(B) Have a round robin sharing so other teachers can give advice from their own successes.
(C) Schedule an extra session for all who want to learn strategies for classroom management.
(D) Explain to these floundering teachers that they will be assessed on their classroom management by their principal, and give them several books to read that should help them.

20. Mr. Adams is principal of Lincoln fifth-and sixth-grade center. The teachers in grade 5 have come to him with a proposal for a unit that would last a month, satisfy learning standards across content areas, and provide a real-life experience for students that would also enhance the strengths of each student in a personal way. It would be a different way to teach but incorporate the students, community, and families in the process. They show him their plans and note the standards being addressed in each part and how it incorporates social, emotional, and academic learning.

Mr. Adams will take the following steps in making this decision. After reviewing the steps, choose the correct answer that puts the steps into the most effective order of action.

I. Observe and assess the management of the unit, the learning outcomes, and student engagement.
II. Analyze the activities and how they align with the standards, support the rigor of the curriculum, and promote student success.
III. Meet with the fifth-grade teachers to ascertain their roles, confidence, and commitment to the unit.
IV. Monitor that teachers are in communication with parents before, throughout, and after the unit is complete.

V. Choose the answer that lists these actions in the order for most effective outcomes.
   (A) III, II, IV, I
   (B) II, IV, III, I
   (C) II, III, IV, I
   (D) I, II, III, IV

21. The new science textbook adoption committee from Carver High School has, in the past, consisted of district personnel and teachers. Over the years parents have been adamant that they are not happy with the current text. As the administrator of curriculum and instruction, and the development of processes in textbook adoption, you want to get parents on board to eliminate the wall of distrust and anger that has been built.
    What action would be most effective in addressing this situation?

    (A) Make sure yourself that the text is culturally acceptable.
    (B) Invite parents to be part of the selection process, giving them a chance to review and express their opinions to the committee.
    (C) Let the committee narrow the textbooks down to two choices and then allow the parents to determine the final choice.
    (D) Take the parent comments that have been made to the committee and tell them that whatever textbook they adopt, it needs to address these issues.

22. At Edison Middle School, Mrs. Bond has had several complaints from parents that the social studies test given by Mrs. Gibbs does not match what has been taught. You conference with Mrs. Gibbs and ask her about this. She doesn't seem to understand what exactly spurs the complaints. You put into motion a plan of action that includes the following:

    I.   Meet with Mrs. Gibbs before each unit to assess the standards she will teach, the methods she will use, and the outcomes she wants the students to have.
    II. Schedule a conference between Mrs. Gibbs and the district curriculum and instruction administrator to share different strategies for assessment.
    III. Observe Mrs. Adams both formally and informally to assess her ability to teach the standards that will be assessed.
    IV. Ask Mrs. Adams to do some self-reflection by taping her own teaching and watching it to learn her own strengths and weaknesses.
    V.   Which order is the most effective for this plan of action?
         (A) II, I, IV, III
         (B) III, II, IV, I
         (C) IV, III, II, I
         (D) I, II, III, IV

23. The state scores arrive and Ms. Penn, the administrator of Washington Elementary School, has concerns about the math scores. State scores have dipped in several areas. To insure the teachers repair the deficit in student learning in these areas, Ms. Penn realizes that she has to have a plan in place at the beginning of the year

that will give teachers a chance to match the unmet standards with specific students and to develop a plan of action to rectify this.

Which of the following would be the best practice for teachers to make such identification?

(A) Have teachers examine the data and write down the name of every student who did not meet AYP in math.

(B) Have teachers sit down and examine each student's detailed scores and analyze the specific standard any student did not meet and a list of specific students who did not meet those standards.

(C) Have teachers examine the scores and choose the top three unmet standards for focused reteaching.

(D) Analyze the unmet standards yourself and give the list to the teachers to save their time.

24. Teachers in Washington Middle School are overprotective of their curriculum, and if they see another grade-level teaching a unit that overlaps with their standards, they complain. To make teachers more aware that overlapping content and standards are designed to flow from one grade level to the next, the administrator designs a professional development session to address this concern.

Which of the following activities will be most effective in addressing this concern?

(A) Have teachers make a list of what they teach and if there is an overlap, decide which will teach what and stick to that.

(B) Have teachers share their units and explain that overlapping is an effective way to instruct for best practice.

(C) Show a video on how teachers can be more effective when they work together than when they work against each other.

(D) Have teachers bring the required standards and objectives for their level and create a diagram that shows how each standard's goals and objectives are meant to overlap and in this way give support. Explain that teaching the same concepts in different ways that are age appropriate is the key.

25. Your school suffered through a student suicide. You want to create some way to become more in touch with all students, supporting them emotionally as well as academically. Your school has clubs, assemblies, spirit weeks, and a student-mentoring student plan. But personally, you feel out of the loop of student well-being.

What direction should your school take to create more opportunities of change in order to correct this?

(A) Spend more time sitting with students in the lunch room.

(B) Develop a student task force to meet with you on a weekly basis to communicate student issues and the undercurrents of the school and to build positive student leaders.

(C) Call students into your office each day, one at a time, and just have a conversation with them.

(D) Set up a big event to take the student's minds off the suicide of a fellow student.

26. Dr. Phillips is the administrator of a middle school in his district. He feels his students are beyond his reach emotionally. His time is limited, he is out of the school attending meetings often, and he would like the situation to change. He sets a goal for himself.

    Which of the following would be the most effective goal in this situation?

    (A) By the end of the year, I will recognize and know something important about 25 percent of the school population.
    (B) By the end of the year, I will have eaten lunch in the cafeteria, sitting at various tables, 100 days.
    (C) By the end of the year, I will form a student committee to meet with me and confer about activities and listen to their opinions, on five different occasions.
    (D) By the end of the year, I will have participated in three planned student field trips.

27. A middle school spends lots of energy widely supporting sports teams. Students who have strengths in academics, arts, music, and other areas are ignored. You are interviewed for the principal's job for this school, and the group conducting the interview asks how you would correct this situation.

    Which of the following would be what an effective leader might reply?

    (A) I would have a talent show and allow any student to perform.
    (B) I would increase communication about programs in the school other than sports.
    (C) I would highlight various students on a large bulletin board citing their strengths with pictures about the various activities in which they are involved.
    (D) I would pull together a team of teachers, students, and parents to work together toward closing this gap.

28. An administrator in a high school has noticed there are several students who have recently made public their alternative sexual lifestyle in dress and behavior.

    What is the most effective thing you can do to demonstrate that an acceptance of these students is expected from teachers and other students?

    (A) Get pamphlets that are published that explain about the Lesbian, Gay, Bisexual, Transgender (LGBT) community and pass them out, encouraging students to get to know these kids better.
    (B) Develop classes on the lifestyle of those who choose this lifestyle.
    (C) Have an assembly supporting these students and invite them to speak.
    (D) Engage in a discrete campaign to promote respect of all people regardless of race, ethnicity, disability, or sexual orientation.

29. In a community survey, 60 percent of those taking the survey expressed concern about the schools meeting the social and emotional needs of the students. In light of those results the middle school set a goal to eliminate this concern. Their goal stated that by the end of the new school year, the spring survey would demonstrate less than five percent still concerned about this issue. A committee was formed that included teachers, staff, parents, community leaders, and students. Due to the size of their group, the principal suggested they divide the group into three parts,

one to target adult-student relationships, one to target student-peer relationships, and the third to target school-community relationships. The question now was how to divide the group.

Which of the following would the principal deem the most effective grouping?

(A) He suggested they keep the community leaders and parents to work on school-community relationships, teachers and other staff to focus on adult-student relationships, and students and teachers to work on peer relationships.

(B) The principal suggested each of the three groups should retain a third of the group with the same diverse mixture of members.

(C) The principal thought the best way would be to randomly select the group members to be nonbiased.

(D) He suggested that the members of the group should choose which area to work in.

30. Cather Elementary School found their disciplinary referrals to the office had increased in the last three years at a rate of 25 percent each year. The administrator who was in charge of discipline knew they had to come up with a way to turn this around. The old strategies were not effective.

Which of the following will be most effective in making this change?

(A) Examine the data and set up a meeting with specialized staff to work with the students whose behavior appears to be unmanageable, to relieve the general education staff from wasting so much classroom time. The referrals can then be made to the resource teacher who knows how to handle such issues.

(B) Call in all the parents of the young offenders and discuss the issues as a group. Have the data ready to distribute and invite some community professionals who could support the parents on effective parenting.

(C) Meet with teachers, examine the data and discuss what steps the school could take to reduce classroom behavioral issues, set a new goal for increasing appropriate student behavior, and develop a plan of action in support of both students and teachers.

(D) Put together a pamphlet that lists opportunities for parenting classes and behavioral health clinics and increase communication with the parents of the students.

31. The teachers at Pillsbury Elementary School have requested that the library be open to their classes at all times and to do away with "library" as a special. The librarian wants the school to continue with the way they've always done it. She feels she is the best person to teach the children how to use the library and its resources. Though a library class is not mandated by the district, years ago it was suggested.

Which of the following statements describes a scenario that is the most ethical and professional as a response to this situation?

(A) Tell the librarian that she will have to work with the teachers since they outnumber her; however, they will have to engage in teaching their own students about the library and its resources.

(B) Tell the teachers that the district encouraged this years ago and hasn't come out with the suggestion that a change is the best practice, so it will be left as it is for now.

(C) Call both sides into the office to find out more details about why the teachers really want this change.

(D) Pull together the leadership committee to gather information, how library use fits in with the school's vision, and what the pros and cons of having it as a special are, and come up with a recommendation that is supported by the data to then make the final decision.

32. Mrs. Carr is the administrator of Apache High School, which has a 50/50 mix of veteran and brand new teaching staff. Mrs. Carr sets up a mentor system between the new and veteran teachers, who volunteer, with assignments to meet once a week, to develop a list of strengths and weaknesses for both teachers, personal class management plans, favorite teaching strategies, and biggest concerns. Mrs. Carr requests that it doesn't matter when or where or how long they meet, but each week they must communicate at least one list with responses from all teachers in their groups. These four concepts will cycle through the year. In other words, every month they should be turning in a list about one of these four areas of teacher skills.

Which of the following is the main reason Mrs. Carr chose this method for mentoring in her school?

(A) It takes time to mentor a teacher and the work should be divided among the staff.

(B) She knows if she doesn't require a report of some kind, there will be teachers who won't meet.

(C) She wants to have the new teachers supported and developing relationships with the veteran teachers to retain as many as possible.

(D) Her veteran teachers need to remember what it was like to be a new teacher.

33. In his informal evaluations, the administrator keeps a collection of notes about interesting methods or resources teachers use in their classrooms that others should know about. He writes a note after those walk-throughs to each teacher and makes a request that they demonstrate that specific teaching strategy at a future teacher meeting or professional development session and asks them if he could put them on a list to do the same at another school in the district.

The administrator knows that

(A) Teachers like and need to share what they do.

(B) Teachers need to learn more about what their fellow teachers are doing in the classroom.

(C) It makes the faculty meetings have more substance.

(D) It develops the leadership capacity of the teachers.

34. In the teacher's lounge of Humphrey Elementary, the administrator put up a professional sharing bulletin board. On it she made a square for each teacher and requested that anytime a teacher read a professional item, article, research, or book it be written on a card and pinned to the board. Each time a teacher

completed a class or was actively involved in anything that contributed to personal or professional development they were to write it on a card and pin it. This included time spent keeping physically fit. The title of the board would be "Improve your professional and personal life balance."

How will this board most effectively influence others?

(A) It will make them more competitive.
(B) It will show who is working to make improvements and who is not.
(C) It will encourage teachers to pay attention to and self-evaluate their work-life balance with something to compare it to.
(D) Teachers will be able to see what they all have in common.

35. Mr. Campbell was required to hold weekly faculty meetings, which were barely tolerated by his staff. He decided that in the new school year he would require every teacher to participate as a small group or individually to share something they learned from professional development, an educational article, or a new strategy they might use in the classroom. He had only one rule. No teacher could use the same method of presentation as any teacher before them.

What is the most effective result from this method?

(A) Increased interest in faculty meetings
(B) Creating buy-in to the faculty meetings
(C) Teacher leadership, increased leaning, and differentiation in teaching styles
(D) Relieving Mr. Campbell to have more time

36. In the past few years, due to the economy of the small town, there are feelings of despair that affect the school. Teacher morale has flagged, there is little parent interaction, and student scores are beginning to drop. As the principal of the combined middle and high school, you recognize that your leadership demands action.

Which of the following would demonstrate leadership?

(A) Start by getting your own attitude and behaviors in line with the vision of academic success, student learning, and community pride.
(B) Suggesting to the mayor they should have a community festival.
(C) Hold a pep assembly and hire an inspirational speaker.
(D) Ask teachers to increase student homework and get a plant for the main office.

37. It is the end of the first quarter and there are many students who have a D or an F in several classes.

As the principal of the school, what is your responsibility?

(A) You need to understand why those students are falling behind already and what is being done by the staff to support these students. You have a responsibility to each student to see that he or she is academically successful.
(B) You are responsible for the faculty doing what they are supposed to do. It is the teacher's job and responsibility to do something to support this student and you need to trust your staff will do what is right.

(C) You are responsible for student success, but if students refuse to study and make bad grades, it is their parents who are ultimately responsible for that. If they don't like the students' grades, let them call and come in and you will find out why the child does not study more at home.

(D) It is the student's responsibility to do the work and study so he or she will get passing grades. If students fail, you need to talk to them and let them know that you expect them to bring up their grades, but ultimately it is on them.

38. Other teachers have complained about Mr. Jones's math classroom being out of control. As his direct administrator you have visited his room for evaluation purposes and always found it to appear to be an appropriate class.

The following is a list of responses the administrator will take. In which order should the following actions occur?

I. Have a conversation with Mr. Jones and ask him if he feels he has the appropriate behavior management skills to be effective, and know what system he uses.
II. Plan several surprise visits to Mr. Jones's class.
III. Evaluate the assessment scores of his students over the past few years and compare them to his colleagues' student scores.
IV. Make a final determination if Mr. Jones is handling his class well or not and address the specific situation.
    (A) I, II, III, IV
    (B) I, III, II, IV
    (C) II, I, III, IV
    (D) III, II, I, IV

39. As the administrator of Hawthorne Middle School, you deal with students who are sent to the office during class time for inappropriate or disruptive behaviors. One teacher has begun sending students down who don't bring a pencil to class. Many of these students have been diagnosed with ADHD or borderline personality disorder. You have spoken to the students about the importance of taking materials to class and even helped them develop new organizational methods, though they don't always work. There are days when the teacher sends three to five students down a day. This is time when the students need to be in class and it is apparent that this behavioral management tactic is not working to increase the behavior the teacher wants. You recognized the behavior that must be addressed is not the students' behavior but the teacher's behavior.

What is the best way to confront this issue with the teacher?

(A) Put pencils in the teacher's box with a note that tells him the school will provide pencils to any student who fails to get to class with one.

(B) Call the teacher into your office for a private conversation and discuss the necessity that each child needs support in different ways and the vision of the school is to do whatever it takes to help children find academic success. In addition, the school will provide any supplies a child needs to be able to be academically successful.

(C) Talk to other teachers and find out how they handle this situation and ask if they will share that with this teacher.

(D) Put the teacher on evaluation for increasing classroom management skills.

40. At the local high school, the principal has heard teachers often remark that they have no clue what happens in other classroom each day. You introduce a new policy that was given approval by the superintendent. Each teacher will spend one day a year with another teacher in another content area, in planning and teaching that other class. The teacher who is the visiting teacher will leave her classes to do team activities with the other team of teachers. The regular teacher will observe and make notes. At the end of each day, you will video record your reflections together. At the end of the year, the short reflections will be played back.

What does this policy support?

(A) Providing opportunities to collaborate, examine others' practices, and build collective learning skills.

(B) Providing a teacher with a varied experience.

(C) Making others aware of how your teaching methods compare with their own.

(D) Demonstrating to students that as teachers you are continually learning.

41. The administrator at Hawthorn Elementary had an area set up in the media center for professional materials with a check-out system. The teachers found this to be confining because there were ongoing classes working there and no room to spread out, discuss, or work. The teachers asked the administrator if he could help them have a place that would offer more convenience for professional learning and collaboration. He was enthusiastic the teachers had such a need and wanted to support them in the most effective and cost-prohibitive way.

Out of the possible choices below, which one would have the most positive impact for the staff, his building, and the need?

(A) Have the teachers meet with the media staff to figure out how to work out the issues.

(B) Call the district operations head and ask him to meet with you and the teachers to figure out the right space at a prohibitive cost.

(C) Keep it simple and let them use part of the teacher's lounge.

(D) Tell the teachers to wait until the summer and he will make it happen.

42. Ms. Carpenter wants to develop Caesar Chavez Middle School's goal to increase more positive interaction and collaboration with families of their students. Before the year begins, she wants to come up with several ideas to make this happen.

What would be the most effective first step?

(A) Schedule an open hour on the day before school begins.

(B) Set up a series of parent-staff events to take place throughout the year.

(C) Ask teachers what they want to do.

(D) Ask parents and teachers what they would like to see happen.

43. The office of Chavez High School is a large open space with students, parents, and staff collecting there before and after school. It is also used as a walk-through

to teacher mailboxes, the lounge, and adult-only restrooms. Between the phones ringing and attending to needs, the office is often congested and chaotic. Dr. Porter, the administrator, wants to change this atmosphere into a more welcoming place for families to enter and to assist them in their efforts to try and approach him personally.

Which of the following actions will have the biggest impact in creating accessibility to Dr. Porter's office for family and community members?

(A) Have the teachers use a door further down the hall unless they actually need direct access to the office personnel.
(B) Add student assistants in the office at the busiest time of the day to help deal with nonpersonal issues.
(C) Put up a number machine for those wanting to see the principal to keep track of the order of requests for a meeting with Dr. Porter.
(D) Rearrange the area with a portable wall that keeps student requests on one side and parents who want to see the principal on the other side.

44. As a new principal at the community's only high school, you are told the previous administration left some negative feeling in the community. The school board assures the new principal that the vision of the school is to be a presence in the community to develop stronger support for students. The new principal is required to come up with a plan on how he will work toward this goal. He makes a list of several actions he could take, but he has to narrow his list down.

Which of the following lists would be the most effective set of actions to develop productive relationships with the community?

(A) Increase all methods of communication, set up home visits, have teachers make home calls to students whose grades are below average each week, and set an open house.
(B) Join the community chamber of commerce, get surveys into the hands of the parents to find out what they see as community strengths and needs, attend community events, volunteer for community events, and use community resources in the school.
(C) Invite parents to a town hall type of meeting to voice their concerns and to get a feel for what they want, talk to parents about getting involved in the school through the PTO, develop a weekly newsletter, and invite parents to come in any time.
(D) Get official data about the community to analyze, visit various churches, volunteer at a community shelter, send home frequent e-mails with information about events at school, and let the parent know how to get in touch with him.

45. The vision of the school where you are an administrator is to engage in meaningful activities with families of the community. As an effective leader, you communicate to community members that the school is a resource that they should take advantage of.

Which of the following is an inappropriate use of the school as a resource?

(A) Church services

(B) Boy Scout events

(C) Community basketball games

(D) School materials

46. You are an administrator in a district whose funds have been cut back and your community has put a bond issue on the ballot to raise taxes for improving buildings. Because the community use of the schools is great, you want to make sure the people are aware of the vote and what it entails.

    Which of the following is the most effective action you can take?

    (A) Go door to door and hold personal conversations.
    (B) Communicate in various ways to all voters and ask those who use the school to collaborate in this work.
    (C) Send out an e-mail in support of the tax.
    (D) Ask teachers to join you in a public rally to promote a yes vote for the tax.

47. Mr. Jay is the principal of the local high school, and with cutbacks getting deeper every year, he is brainstorming with his staff and community social, religious, and business leaders on how to best meet some of the most urgent needs of their children. They come up with ideas and create focus committees to move forward with some of these ideas.

    Based on the work Mr. Jay is putting into this effort, what can be said about his values and beliefs?

    (A) Mr. Jay believes that taking care of the urgent needs of students is directly supportive of academic goals.
    (B) Mr. Jay believes in being a leader and works hard to take charge.
    (C) Mr. Jay values his teachers and his school.
    (D) Mr. Jay values the students and understands the school is only one part of a community that must work together.

48. The Parent Teacher Organization (PTO) at Harmony Middle School is not functioning well. Most parents work, and those few who don't work have not taken any initiative to be in partnership with the school in reaching its goals.

    Which of the following statements is the thought of a leader who will be effective in helping a school develop core values?

    (A) The parents probably are not aware of the importance of their partnership with the school and need training.
    (B) As a leader who wants the most and best student support in academics, community affairs, and life, you know you must advocate for the students and help parents see the importance of the shared vision and the difference they can make in their child's life through the PTO.
    (C) The parents in this district have too many other things to worry about and really don't need to spend time having a PTO. If we just eliminate the group, everyone would be relieved.
    (D) The PTO at South Middle School functions extremely well. Maybe I could get some of those parents to come over here and show our parents how it is done.

49. Mrs. Taylor is the principal of an elementary school in an urban area that is wealthy and harbors many "helicopter" parents. In the past the parents have volunteered to be in the school for various reasons, but too many times it results in a parent interfering with their child's classroom because of their need to hover. This isn't healthy for the child, the class, or the parent. Mrs. Taylor knows it is time to make some changes.

Which of the following statements in a letter would be most effective in bringing this practice of hovering to a halt?

   (A) Starting this year, all volunteers are required to stay in the area that has been assigned to them within the school as a requisite for keeping the job.
   (B) Parents who want to make contact with their child during school hours are now required to ask the office staff who will summon your child to the office.
   (C) There will be no more volunteers used in our building.
   (D) Volunteers who have children in the school are banned from going into any classroom while they are volunteering.

50. In Samuel Adams Elementary, Mrs. Jamal, principal, was confronted by several teachers requesting money to take the children bowling to celebrate the students' great test scores. They feel that they have to ask too many times for parents to send money and the school is in a low socioeconomic status area. Mrs. Jamal gives them the money and moves her budget around.

Which answer is the best basis for Mrs. Jamal to determine this idea was worth funding over other things?

   (A) It fit into supporting the vision of the school and the money would be spent directly on the students, whose hard work had contributed to making the vision successful.
   (B) Mrs. Jamal understood that children need to have some fun after working hard.
   (C) Mrs. Jamal knows the children are poor and rarely get opportunities to go bowling.
   (D) This action will let the teachers know that she supports what they feel is important.

51. Mr. Rydel learned to be a mediator in his classes while attaining a degree in education administration. During his first years as a principal in a middle school, he grew quite effective at it. He has used it between two students, two teachers, and a parent and teacher. This year he's noticed that teacher and student conflict has grown, so he decides to apply what he knows to mediate a conflict between a teacher and a student.

Which of the following is NOT a reason to use mediation?

   (A) To be fair.
   (B) To allow both parties a respectable format for airing grievances.
   (C) To find out how this issue can be averted in the future.
   (D) To gain control.

52. The superintendent has requested the principal and one teacher from each school to attend a community group that deals with child abuse in the community. He would like for them to each be prepared to answer questions about the role of a school in child abuse.

    What is the best reason for a principal to attend this event?

    (A) To get to know more people in the community and let them know he is open to helping them.
    (B) To support the success of all children in the community and to demonstrate the value of the community and school working together on all issues that affect student success.
    (C) To find out which children are abused at home so he can be more aware and keep teachers and staff informed.
    (D) He has been asked by the superintendent and he knows that by going it will help him get higher ratings on his evaluation.

53. In the new school year, to avert the huge issue with cell phones in the classroom, Mr. Jones at Truman High has worked with the teachers in his building to formulate effective ways they can put them to use. They will also discuss national student cell phone issues in the first five seminar classes. The teachers have created ways to incorporate the apps, the camera, and the ability to get on the Internet within lessons. Students who are found to be using phones for illicit purposes will be sent to the office, where the phone will be held in a locked cabinet for 72 hours before being returned. He has parental support and district support.

    The school hopes to reduce teacher-student conflict, put responsibility on students to attend to lessons, and make clear the consequence for inappropriate use.

    What is the most effective result Mr. Jones hopes to see by making this attempt to make cell phone use fit into the class lessons?

    (A) The ability of teachers to actively and intentionally use technology that is in the hands of most students.
    (B) Parents will be happier that we are allowing them in the classroom without fear of them being taken away.
    (C) To keep students from being sent to the office for having a cell phone in the classroom.
    (D) Teachers will have less conflict with students.

54. The Jefferson School administrator has decided to increase professional development throughout the year in areas of the lowest state test scores. They want to give teachers every advantage to effectively teach these skills across the content in an effort to increase student learning.

    How will the administrator of Jefferson School know if the professional development is making a difference?

    (A) Have teachers fill out a pre- and posttest to see how much they learned.
    (B) Have teachers fill out a pre- and post-survey to find out how much they thought the professional development helped them in their teaching.
    (C) Look at grades at the end of each quarter and see if they improve.

(D) Use the state scores given at the end of the year for improvement in those targeted skill areas.

55. Mr. Jones is constantly handing out short surveys and polls and asking questions of teachers to maintain the course toward promotion of the core values of the school and developing short talks for each faculty meeting based on this feedback.

Using this method to continually evaluate and promote the core values is largely ineffective for which of the following reasons?

(A) Teachers will become bored with it after a while and their answers may not be good data.
(B) Data needed for a good evaluation requires various sources.
(C) Mr. Jones will find that he has created too much work for himself.
(D) The surveys should be given to students as well.

56. As the new principal at Monroe Elementary school, Mrs. Bond has the task of bringing the community, families, and school personnel together to commit to improving increased student attendance, parent participation in parent-teacher meetings, and school readiness. She has developed a list of actions that she can take over the next three years toward these improvements.

Mrs. Bond makes a list of the following actions that she can do over the three years.

I. Write a regular column in the school's newsletter that is sent home monthly, send it to be published in the local newspaper, and send his column to the leaders of community organizations with information that directly addresses these issues and how the community and school can work together to make improvements.
II. Call a series of town hall–type meetings in the school library to present resources to families in support of a focus on improving these areas.
III. Meet with town and business leaders to share with them the school's vision for improving readiness, attendance, and parent participation.
IV. Have conversations on a regular basis with the children in their homeroom class about these issues.
V. Which of these actions could she begin even before school starts in the fall?
(A) I, II, III, IV
(B) I, II, IV
(C) Only IV
(D) I, II, III

57. The Middle School in Smithtown has a school vision for continual school improvement. This year the staff has come together to decide what to focus on. As the administrator you lead them through the process of evidence-based inquiry.

Which of the following is the proper cycle for successful evidence-based inquiry?

(A) Analyze the problem, state it, develop specific and measureable goals, take action.

(B) Make a problem statement, define specific and measureable goals, make a plan, follow the plan, analyze.

(C) State the problem, analyze it, develop specific and measureable goals, plan, take action.

(D) Track the problem for a specific period, put it into a problem statement, analyze it, set goals, make plans, take action.

58. As the administrator of a local elementary school you want your staff to be aware of emerging educational trends and what the research says about these trends to keep in mind when developing school improvement goals.

   What is the most effective method to assess and develop the skills of your staff for this purpose?

   (A) Require teachers send you a digital copy of a report on a recent trend they've read and researched.

   (B) Sign up volunteers to present at staff meetings, a recent trend, and what the research says about it.

   (C) Meet with teachers in small groups and discuss current trends and research.

   (D) Find a speaker to bring in for professional development to discuss trends and what the research says.

59. At Jefferson Middle School, the staff have worked for years on various school improvement goals. As a new administrator in the building, you feel there is little coordination between the goals, the actions that are planned, and the programs offered by the school.

   Which of the following will be the most helpful in presenting your findings to the staff?

   (A) Develop a PowerPoint that reviews the history of the goals and their success.

   (B) Have a discussion about these goals at the first staff development meeting to get a feel for the coherency of them and the action plans that were followed.

   (C) Make a large visual to show the goals, the evidence of success, and how they do or do not relate to each other and the programs of the school.

   (D) Throw out all old goals and start anew.

60. As the principal of Mitchell Middle school, you notice that the attendance rate has been below the district average for the last three years. Your superintendent is not pleased and wants you to raise the rate. The school has a high population of free and reduced lunch, and is located near several low-income housing developments. What would be the best course of action to take to increase student attendance?

   (A) Talk with the students about why they are not coming to school.

   (B) Make home visits with the social worker to inform parents it is their responsibility to make sure their children come to school.

   (C) Notify parents every time a student is absent.

   (D) Create a committee of teachers, parents, community members, and students to look at possible causes and develop some action steps to increase the attendance rate.

61. A local newspaper has published a series of articles suggesting that your Varsity Boys Basketball Team's recent state championship is tainted due to reports that ineligible and illegal players participated during the season.

    Which of the following options would be the best strategy to deal with this situation?

    (A) Write a rebuttal editorial or letter to the editor that refutes all of the allegations listed in the article and supports the athletic director and coach.
    (B) Contact the editor of the paper and complain about the damage that these articles have caused to your school as they are based upon rumor and innuendo.
    (C) Immediately conference with the head coach and athletic director and ask them to launch an internal investigation to get to the truth.
    (D) Contact the district athletics director and superintendent to begin an investigation into these claims.

62. An article is published in the local newspaper, which includes several quotes from five of your teachers employed at your high school. The article and the quotes from the teachers are very critical of the school and school district's response to a recent upswing in gang activity and violence. The paper does not contact you or any other member of the district administration for a quote of information.

    Which of the following is an appropriate response to this situation?

    (A) Contact the paper and request that they send a reporter to your school to interview you and get the district administration's side of the story.
    (B) Call the teachers in and remind them that negative comments like these may lead to punitive action. Tell them they are not district spokesman and should not comment.
    (C) Take no action as these quotes are protected free speech as outlined in the U.S. Constitution.
    (D) Respond to the article with a letter to the editor, which you write after getting district permission.

63. The Midland High School principal received notice that the chronically low student test score will lead to mandated state intervention. Next year an academic assistance team and a principal mentor from the State Department of Education will assume leadership and supervision of the school in all academic and instructional areas. Several significant changes have been made, and parents, students, and the community are very concerned about what is going on and what will happen to their children. In addition, personnel changes will be made, which may either remove or reassign some teachers in and out of the school.

    What is the best strategy to address these concerns and inform all concerned parents, students, and community?

    (A) Post all of the information on the school's website for parents to read.
    (B) Hold a school-wide assembly for students to inform them of the changes.
    (C) Schedule a series of parent/community forums to discuss the changes.
    (D) Send out an automated call to all parents followed with a detailed newsletter.

64. At a community forum to address new school reforms efforts, the principal has developed a brochure that outlines the major points of the school-wide initiatives. Horatio Middle school has a significant number of Latino students who have limited English language skills and are also low income. The new plan requires that all parents select supplementary services for their children if they are failing. seventy percent of African American parents returned them, while only 20 percent of Latino parents have submitted their choice for their child's services. The brochure was written in English as well as Spanish.

   Which of these could most likely be the reason that Latino parents did not respond to the survey?

   (A) It is possible that some Latino parents may be illiterate and unable to read even in their native language.

   (B) It is a proven fact that poor and limited-language parents do not care about their child's education.

   (C) The Latino parents do not believe that their children need the supplementary services as they are not necessary for them to be successful.

   (D) The Latino students did not want to disappoint their parents by giving them the information, and therefore, many of the parents did not receive the information.

65. At a high school that has had chronically low test scores, the principal has been tasked with developing a new vision.

   Which is the most effective first step in selecting the committee members to formulate the vision statement?

   (A) Contact district administration and ask them to select representatives from central office to participate on the committee.

   (B) Develop a written, concrete plan that will be followed to select committee members as well as participation parameters.

   (C) Formulate a list of potential participants by meeting with the PTA president, superintendent, and department chairs from the school.

   (D) Ask the school-based administrators to formulate a list of five to seven possible committee members.

CONSTRUCTED-RESPONSE ESSAY QUESTION (CR)

Question1: A new principal is hired at Fredrick Douglass Elementary School. The school is an underresourced urban elementary school. The teachers are overworked, but they care a lot about what they do. Most of the parents work two jobs and do not have time to invest in their children's learning. The students at Susan B. Anthony Elementary School just outside of the city have five times the number of students above reading level by the third grade than Fredrick Douglass Elementary School. The school has a limited budget, but the city mayor has just started an educational campaign called "Tune in and Read"; they are offering funding to schools with the greatest need but also the most practical program proposals to make the most difference.

   What are three types of programs that the new principal can propose so that Fredrick Douglass Elementary School can improve the reading level of its students?

Appendix 1

Practice Test One

Answers

1. C	23. B	45. D
2. B	24. D	46. B
3. D	25. B	47. D
4. A	26. A	48. B
5. C	27. D	49. B
6. C	28. D	50. A
7. D	29. B	51. D
8. B	30. C	52. B
9. C	31. D	53. B
10. C	32. C	54. C
11. D	33. D	55. B
12. B	34. C	56. D
13. B	35. C	57. B
14. A	36. A	58. C
15. D	37. A	59. C
16. B	38. D	60. D
17. D	39. B	61. D
18. A	40. A	62. C
19. B	41. B	63. C
20. C	42. D	64. A
21. B	43. D	65. B
22. A	44. B	

Appendix 1

Practice Test One

Answer Explanations

1. The correct answer is (C). It will be important for the new principal to establish an effective relationship with the parents, students, and teachers in the plan and seek some commitment from these stakeholders, in the development of a shared vision, with goals and objectives before any plan is developed.—Standard 4.f

2. The correct answer is (B). All stakeholders must have their opinions heard and have a part in how their school might meet this part of the district vision.—Standard 1.a

3. The answer is (D). The teacher's behavior was unprofessional and went against the vision of the district. The teachers are either incapable or indolent in their classrooms.—Standard 1.c

4. The answer is (A). It will take leadership to support the vision of the school as well as a total community and staff buy-in to find academic success. To look for possible support at the same time staying focused on the positive will create an atmosphere for change.—Standard 1.g

5. The correct answer is (C). Requesting more to hire subs is only a temporary solution, as this collaboration should be sustained for the long term not for just one year. Asking teachers to stay after school for one hour is sometimes a breach of contract especially if the contract does not specify that the teachers are required to be in the school for an extra hour, not only that most teachers have grading and lesson planning to complete after school. This would only add to their heavy workload. The best answer is C as it allows for the principal to work with all those affected by the school schedule to come up with the same time to meet and have the specials classes.—Standard 1.d

6. The correct answer is (C). Sending a letter out and requesting they all reply, with those who have a passion for this task meeting to work on it, opens the field for everyone to have a part, for some to take more leadership with him, and others to opt out if they so choose. It also sets the tone for relationships with the staff that you are open to them but understanding that their time is important, and it provides an added opportunity for those who are more driven to lead in this area.—Standard 1.c

7. The correct answer is (D). When talking to personnel about behavioral issues, it should always be done individually even though the same talk applies to many. You have to lead. It is often difficult to do the right thing. People may not like you, but that is not the issue. You have to stop unethical behaviors in your school.—Standard 2.a

8. The answer is (B). You have to confront the issue but with empathy of the teachers' situation. Telling them that you too are in the dark and as soon as you know, you will tell them and you will also get someone right away to answer questions about who would have to move or if it will be a choice.—Standard 2.b

9. The answer is (C). Using opportunities that happen in real life is the most effective teaching tool a teacher can use. To give the teachers permission to do this and encourage the students to examine this issue will help them understand each other more. You can't control what parents do, but you can teach the children. Take advantage of it.—Standard 2.d

10. The answer is (C). The purpose of the workshop was to raise student reading levels, so the only way to evaluate the effectiveness of the workshops in raising student reading scores is to look at student reading scores both before the teachers learned better methods and after.—Standard 2.e

11. The inappropriate response is (D). It is never appropriate to move problem teachers to another school as a punishment. If they are a capable and professional teacher, put them on evaluation or work to correct the situation. If they are not capable or unprofessional, fire them.—Standard 2.f

12. The answer is (B). Before anything happens, it should be determined which specific items will be targeted throughout the three years. Then you are ready to gather your task force and share information and establish goals and objectives. After that, you are ready to form committees and brainstorm events and activities and then you are ready to develop a long-range plan.—Standard 2.b

13. The best answer is (B). The first thing to do would be to meet with a few of the families who feel comfortable, in a social environment with the small leadership team. This will set the attitude of the school as open and welcoming before you have larger events or begin the year.—Standard 3.a

14. The correct answer is (A). This goal involves all stakeholders. What is not seen at school is often noticed by parents. Parents need to be involved in this change.—Standard 3.b

15. The correct answer is (D). The issue is with the general education teachers and they should be addressed, not the para or the resource teacher. You do alert the resource teacher that there might be more need for resources in those classes and you'd like to meet with all of them to discuss possibilities.—Standard 3.c

16. The answer is (B). When a student on an IEP is involved in any incident that may involve his or her disability, a meeting is held to determine if the behavior is a manifestation of his or her disability or not. If it is, then the team proceeds to make decisions about the best way to meet the needs as directed on the IEP with the least restrictions.—Standard 3.d

17. The answer is (D). Effective leaders in education must strive for equity of educational opportunity.—Standard 3.e

18. The answer is (A). This goal does not support any interaction.—Standard 3.f

19. The answer is (B). This would allow others to bring up issues related to classroom management. The goal is to support teachers so as to increase student learning.—Standard 4.c

20. The correct order of action is answer (C). II, Mr. Adams must satisfy that the unit indeed meets with the aligned standards, supports the rigor, and promotes student success in a challenging and efficient manner. III, when he is sure the unit fits the standards and is in line with the vision and goals of the school, he will meet with teachers. IV, during the process he must monitor that the teachers are in communication with all stakeholders throughout, getting and keeping parents on board. I, finally it is imperative that Mr. Adams observe and assess the management of the unit, the results of student learning and engagement.—Standard 4.d

21. The answer is (B). Having parents take part in the process is the most effective way to get their support and that may be as important as the text you select.—Standard 4.a

22. The answer is (A). II, the next step after conferencing with Mrs. Gibbs would be to support her with knowledge on how to assess. I, meet with Mrs. Gibbs to go over her plans for alignment of standards and outcomes. IV, ask her to do self-reflection at this point as she is developing new strategies. III, observe her for improved teaching and assessment of the standards.—Standard 4.f

23. The answer is (B). Teachers should sit down and go through individual student data and examine the unmet and met standards and know exactly which students demonstrated deficits in which areas for best practice.—Standard 4.g

24. The answer is (D). Teachers have to be aware of the continuum of the standards to be effective in their instruction and methods.—Standard 4.b

25. The answer is (B). The development of student leadership is the answer. Students know what is going on and they often are the ones who can make a difference. Meeting with students one on one is not comfortable with most kids but being on a task force with the principal and developing leadership skills would be positive, effective, and keep you in the loop.—Standard 1.a

26. The answer is (A). If the goal is to engage emotionally with students, it will only happen if he knows who the students are and what is important to them.—Standard 5.e

27. The answer is (D). The other ideas have some merit except that they lack stakeholder input. Finding students whose strengths are in leadership to serve is the most effective first step.—Standard 5.b

28. The answer is (D). Without forcing the issue and other than simply modeling respect for all students and teachers, you can begin a simple and slow-building campaign that will focus on respect to others regardless of differences. If done slowly and in the form of respect for all people, you can permeate the minds of students at a deeper level.—Standard 5.a

29. The answer is (B). The principal recognizes that all stakeholders should be included in all groups with a cross-section of those represented in each action group.—Standard 5.d

30. The answer is (C). The problems happen in the classroom, at school, and that is the place to begin. Teachers are directly involved with this problem and will have

to be directly involved in solving it. With the backing of the principal, a plan, and positive supports, behaviors should improve.—Standard 6.d

31. The correct answer is (D). Involving stakeholders in the process of the decision is the most effective way to bring collaboration between the groups, find a best fit solution and one that aligns with the school vision and goals.—Standard 6.f

32. The answer is (C). New teachers often give up teaching after that first and challenging year, when it is after this first year that a teacher really starts to get a grip on teaching. To be able to retain teachers that the district and school have developed along is an effective and positive action.—Standard 6.a

33. The answer is (D). It develops leadership skills of a teacher, and schools need teachers to take leadership position in various capacities within the district.—Standard 6.g

34. The answer is (C). Teachers need to be encouraged to tend to their own learning, improvement, and healthy work-life balance.—Standard 6.h

35. The answer is (C). This would set up an opportunity to develop leadership, increase learning from peers, and demonstrate how to differentiate their styles of teaching.—Standard 6.c

36. The answer is (A). Leaders always begin by making sure that their mind and passion are ready for the challenge. From there they will develop a plan of action, but their own attitude will show others that they are not giving up. They will inspire, motivate, and lead.—Standard 7.b

37. The answer is (A). You are responsible in the end. You need to know why students are failing, not to point fingers or place blame but to figure out how to lead the school toward the goal of academic success.—Standard 7.d

38. The correct answer is (D). Before going to Mr. Jones, find out how his student scores stand up to others in the building. If they are lower, then do some surprise visits to see if you find what you've been told is true or if it is about something else between these staff members and Mr. Jones. If your surprise visits and conversations find he indeed lacks control over his classes, then address the situation.—Standard 7.c

39. The correct answer is (B). Remind a teacher that part of the school's vision is to create an atmosphere that will support every student in whatever manner necessary to maintain learning and increase academic progress. This includes happily providing pencils to those without, as opposed to having them out of class.—Standard 7.e

40. The answer is (A). Teachers jarred from their normal practice will be refreshed while really having to collaborate, examine their own habitual practices, and build their learning skills. Teaching a different content with different students makes a teacher more aware of her own strengths and weaknesses and how to learn and work in a different environment. It will encourage each teacher to open their mind to new avenues and strategies.—Standard 7.g

41. The answer is (B). Anytime space is required to be altered or used in a different way, the operations officer should be part of the plan and he would be the person to collaborate with in making a useful niche for professional development.—Standard 7.a

42. The answer is (D). Since the parent is the biggest stakeholder and the goal is to work with them, they along with the staff should be consulted through various

means of communication to find out what would make parents feel supported and a part of Kennedy Elementary.—Standard 8.b

43. The answer is (D). All of the ideas will help, but creating a more formal space for families who want access to the administrator will send the message that he welcomes them.—Standard 8.a

44. The answer is (B). It is the only one that is focused on the administration's presence out in the community.—Standard 8.d

45. The answer is (D). Materials purchased by the district can be used only for the purpose requested by the schools.—Standard 8.g

46. The answer is (B). Getting the public who also depend on use of the schools to work with you and communicating the message effectively is the most effective action you can take.—Standard 8.i

47. The answer is (D). The school principal understands it is important to involve all stakeholders to ensure school programs are maintained.—Standard 8.j

48. The correct answer is (B). An effective leader knows he needs support from parents, community, staff, and students. He has to step up and advocate for the students and find a way to give the parents more opportunity to become involved.—Standard 9.c

49. The correct answer is (B). It is to the point, does not just single out the volunteers, and is phrased in a positive manner.—Standard 9.e

50. The correct answer is (A). The school principal understands that she needs to support the students and staff when it comes to the hard work of preparing and meeting expectations for standardized assessments. This is an effort that needs to be acknowledged and celebrated as it fosters a cooperative atmosphere as well.—Standard 9.d

51. The answer is (D). Mediation gives control to those in conflict as they are encouraged to find common ground, see a way to resolve disputes, and demonstrate respect to one another. It is not about control.—Standard 9.k

52. The answer is (B). It is important for all student success to be involved in any issues in the community that concern the children and families of the community, and to share his knowledge of school law in this situation.—Standard 9.h

53. The answer is (B). Because cell phones are here to stay and have become so entrenched in everything we do, it is essential that we work with them and not against them and teachers need to learn how to incorporate them successfully in the classroom.—Standard 9.f

54. The correct answer is (C). The principal should continuously see if the professional development is increasing test scores. If not, the principal needs to revisit the professional development and see how it is linked to improving student assessment scores.—Standard 10.a

55. The answer is (B). For continuous improvement in the school, data needs to be collected from various sources to get a well-rounded picture of progress.—Standard 10.b

56. The answer is (D). Each of these could be immediately initiated by Mrs. Bond.—Standard 10.c

57. The answer is (B). The first thing is to come up with a problem and put it into a statement. Then you develop specific and measurable goals toward solving the

problem, make a plan, take action on that plan, and in the end analyze or study the measured objectives.—Standard 10.d

58. The answer is (C). To assess and develop these skills, it will be important that all teachers have more than one chance to display such skills. By having short meetings with a smaller groups of teachers, the administrator will be able to assess individual skills and help develop them.—Standard 10.f

59. The answer is (C). It is valuable for everyone to see how the goals were assessed, how they did or did not work together and with other school programs and services, and present it is a large visual that accurately demonstrates the coordination or lack thereof.—Standard 10.h

60. The answer is (D). The question tests a school leader's knowledge of reasonable practices when faced with a problem that is multifaceted, such as family and community structures. The best response would be to include all stakeholders in understanding the problem and coming up with a solution that involves the school, family, and community. Therefore, (D) is correct; to create a committee of teachers, parents, community members, and students to look at possible causes and develop some action steps to increase the attendance rate.—Standard 3.c

61. The answer is (D). Principals must be able to effectively handle public relations so that when these situations materialize, there must be a plan of action that seeks to address the perceptions of wrongdoings. (A) Writing a rebuttal letter while effective in getting your side of the story out may just fan the flames and lead to additional letters and coverage. (B) Contacting the editor of the paper would lead to the paper believing that they have a story "with legs" that they can continue to investigate. (C) It is important to confer with the head coach and athletic director, but because they are the persons directly in charge of player eligibility, an investigation by them alone may be seen as biased and tainted; therefore, (D) Contact district-level administration to get guidance on what the next step is, and if an investigation is warranted, it should originate from their office. This is aligned with determining, communicating, or enforcing school policies, especially for communicating properly with media outlets.—Standard 2.e

62. The best answer is (C). The court affirmed for the first time that public school teachers do not relinquish their constitutional right to free speech on matters of public concern simply because they work in the public sector (*Pickering v. Board of Education, 1968*). In deciding whether a teacher's First Amendment rights have been violated, a court must weigh the interest of a teacher, as a citizen, to speak out on matters of public concern against the school board's legitimate interest in maintaining the efficiency of the workplace. School districts often establish procedures for dealing with the press and all administrators and teachers are made aware of these guidelines. (A) Requesting the newspaper to send the reporter out to interview you is risky as the interview request may be seen as disingenuous. (B) Calling the teachers in and threatening them with a negative personnel action is illegal and serves to damage the relationship of the schools with the staff and community by appearing to stifle any comment on the subject. (D) Responding to the article with your own letter to the editor is another attempt at getting your side out, but this is best left to district administration, so (C) Civil liberty organizations have several court decisions that support the right for teachers as private citizens to make comments outside of their workplace. Because they made these comments outside of the school work

day and workplace, they are protected by their First Amendment rights. Adjusting methods of family involvement for special populations, that is, low Socio-Economic Status (SES), commuter community, non-English speaking, etc., Standard 3.g states that a school leader should act with cultural competence and responsiveness in their interactions, decision making, and practice.—Standard 3.g

63. The correct answer is (C). It is always important to address the concerns of parents, students, and the community especially when there are significant changes coming very soon. (A) This option does get the information out to the public, but does not allow for any discourse or discussion. It also takes for granted that all parents have daily access to the Internet (B) While it is important to meet with students and talk with them about significant changes, it is never a good decision to talk to them prior to informing parents as this will often lead to more confusion and the information they bring home may be incorrect or incomplete. (D) Sending out an automated call is usually reserved for short announcements that parents can respond to quickly such as bad weather, school closings, and early dismissals. This is not an appropriate way to transmit this type of information, so (C) is the best strategy. This option allows for adequate preparation and offers the parents and community an opportunity to gather information and ask informed questions.—Standard 4.a

64. The answer is (A). Recent research has shown that a significant number of Latino adults who immigrate to this nation are also barely literate in their native language. School districts have started programs that teach Latino students Spanish grammar and language skills. Also several communities have initiated adult literacy programs that teach Latino adults both English and Spanish literacy skills.—Standard 5.f

65. The correct answer is (B). Developing a school vision is a collaborative process that should include parents, teachers, administrators, and other concerned persons. (A) Requesting district administration to select representatives from the central office to participate is un-democratic and would be seen as a top-down bureaucratic move. (C) It is inclusive to ask for input from the PTA and others, but each of them will select persons who they think will push their own agenda. (D) School-based administrators will normally ask those parents who have been both more participative and easy to work with, so (B) Before any selection is made, an objective, well-written, publicly assessable plan must be formulated to insure a level-playing field for nomination and selection.—Standard 1.d

CONSTRUCTED-RESPONSE ANSWER QUESTION ONE:

Scoring CR Question One: Answers should include, but should not be limited to the following:

1. Well-developed analysis and synthesis of all documents, if any, provided
2. Describe challenges faced by the school
3. Evaluation of an improvement plan (strengths and weaknesses)
4. Multiple ways to elicit community support
5. Multiple actions a principal should take

Practice Test Two

Questions

85 Multiple Choice and 1 Constructed Essay

1. Brightenwood Middle school has experienced progressive increases in the number of students transferring out of the program in recent years, even though there is continued growth in the neighborhood.

   Which would be the most effective approach to uncover the cause of the dwindling enrolment?

   (A) Explore the academic and behavioral history of transferring students to uncover any patterns.

   (B) Look for opportunities for educators at more desirable schools to mentor those at Brightenwood.

   (C) Construct a committee to welcome potential students before the transfer lottery opens.

   (D) Form a community task force to study the factors and motivations of departing students.

2. Blue Elementary school has a higher number of special needs learners than the district average, but still receives only 1 Educational Assistant (EA) position for each grade. This has led to a high number of disruptive student outbursts in the hallway, as the available staff cannot manage some of the more active students.

   What suggestions might help effectively manage the disproportionate number of high-needs learners to EAs?

   (A) Implement more in service training for the primary teachers.

   (B) Designate cool-off rooms, where disruptive students can be contained until they calm down.

   (C) Provide an additional space where small groups can meet and the EAs can support the student cooperatively.

   (D) Share details with the staff on when the most common times of day are for each student so they can work to prevent a disruptive episode.

3. At Mountainview High School, the students who are identified as gifted received differential instruction at the level that is right for each participant. This academic level–appropriate instruction is available as independent research projects or faux college entrance tests.

   What is an effective way to improve the gifted instruction in the future?

   (A) Do nothing; the brightest students are highly motivated and will continue to do well.
   (B) Evaluate that the administering of gifted education is in alignment with state standards.
   (C) Allow the gifted identified students to have more time in the library to pursue academic interests.
   (D) Form a team of teachers to mentor the gifted learners.

4. Students at Sunnyview Middle School are allowed to handwrite or type their end-of-the-semester historical biography paper. Sunnyview has a large computer space, but it opens only after school. Nearly 40 percent of students turn in hand-written versions of their lengthy papers.

   How could access to technology be increased to encourage more future-ready students?

   (A) Open the library during recess as well.
   (B) Invite the parents to the after-school hours to type their students' papers.
   (C) Introduce the classrooms to the resources during school hours, allowing in class time to be spent in the computer room.
   (D) Invite the technology teacher into the class to talk about the resources available in the computer room.

5. At Bridgetown Elementary School, an increasing number of upper grade–level students are not meeting state testing benchmarks. Upon further investigating it is determined that some of the same students have been acting out in class and on recess.

   What is an effective way to handle this situation?

   (A) Invite all the affected students to a meeting to discuss obstacles and challenges.
   (B) Construct a school-wide assembly focusing on the importance of determination.
   (C) Ask for help from an expert from the office for gifted learning from the district or state level.
   (D) Solicit input from current research, teachers, gifted students, and their parents to develop a plan.

6. A kindergartener at Big Red Primary School is being evaluated for possibly having learning disabilities or being on the autism spectrum, but no conclusion has been reached yet. The student can often be found crouched to the ground, trying to tie their shoes just right. Sometimes the student's frustration escalates into disruptive outbursts. The skills support specialist keeps packs of no tie lace alternatives at the school.

What should be done in this situation?

(A) Give the special laces to the student.
(B) Wait for evaluation result before deciding.
(C) Do not give the special laces to the student.
(D) Give the special laces to the student and everyone in the class.

7. In Glenn County, the school board will be announcing and enacting boundary changes in the fall without inviting lengthy public input or opinion. A core group of parents who are champions of fundraising and in class volunteering are going to be forced to withdraw when changes take effect.

   What can be done to prevent the loss of such integral school community members?

   (A) Drop hints about upcoming changes to policy and boundaries.
   (B) Confide in a peer about your concerns, but take no action.
   (C) Encourage all parents to attend school board meetings and listen really, really carefully.
   (D) Tell only one parent and ask them not to tell anyone.

8. The assistant principal at Rolling Hills Learning Center has noticed in the last 2 weeks the principal has become increasingly disheveled in appearance and short tempered with the student body. Personally you know that the principal is suffering from a personal issue, which you thought previously to be under control.
   What can be done to improve this?

   (A) Consult with the principal in private to express your concerns.
   (B) Not much.
   (C) Just be overly nice and well dressed to compensate.
   (D) Suggest that the principal work uninterrupted on outlining a long-term project.

9. A teacher of almost 30 years lost her temper with a few parents last week. While totally out of character, she got up close to the faces of the parents of the rowdiest students who come to school every day with a backpack of excuses. While there were no insults or mean words, the teacher did direct those parents to start saying "no" to their kids sometimes. Before the principal was inundated with parent complaints about the interaction, the teacher had fully disclosed the details of the situation.
   What is an effective way to handle this situation?

   (A) Invite all the parents to handwrite their concerns and mail to the superintendent.
   (B) Tell the parents it is being handled.
   (C) Ask the teacher to contact their union rep and hold on for a bumpy ride.
   (D) Inform the parents that the teacher has been talked to and invite them in for conferences to discuss how to align some standards with the teacher.

10. The principal at Hutchins Elementary School likes dogs a lot. Talking about dogs is an easy way to connect with most students, and it makes for a playful environment around the school. At the start of this year, the principal decided to take it

a little bit further and started barking when greeted by the students and parents alike.

Is this acceptable behavior?

(A) Yes, but on a very limited basis.
(B) Yes, everyone likes dogs.
(C) No, it is not professional.
(D) Maybe, it depends on whether it upsets the parents.

11. During a nonschool-related weekend event, a school leader witnesses an assistant principal aggressively pull the hair of their spouse.

How should this be handled?

(A) Tell another professional about what was seen and seek feedback.
(B) Ask the spouse if they are alright.
(C) Confront the assistant principal directly.
(D) Report the incident to the police.

12. This year at the annual school carnival at Roseway Middle School, there will be the addition of a dunk tank. The community will be invited to purchase tickets as a fundraiser in exchange for the chance to throw balls at a target and drop the person on the platform into very cold water. The PTA is asking all teachers and on-site administrators to take a shift in the tank.

Is this acceptable behavior for a school leader?

(A) Never, it is very unprofessional.
(B) Probably not, the parents might complain.
(C) Possible, take a school survey first.
(D) Yes, it serves a school cause.

13. A small number of students at Glencoe Elementary represent a large segment of cultural variety.

What is an effective way to allow these students to feel comfortable and culturally supported?

(A) Hold an all school assembly with any students representing cultural diversity on stage in an open Q&A-type forum.
(B) Form a committee to examine ways the school can become more culturally responsive and intelligent, inviting parents and students representing cultural diversity to join.
(C) Have one diversity day at school every year.
(D) Take no action.

14. At Dovelake K-8 School, there is a yearly winter performance where students sing, perform short skits, and generally entertain the audience. Up until now, the event is decorated in a way that suggests only one holiday is being recognized in the event.

What steps can be taken to make the yearly winter performance more inclusive?

(A) There is no way to include all winter-time celebrations.
(B) Let every participant and audience member bring in decorations they wish to see.

(C) Cancel the event, so no family feels left out.

(D) Distribute a survey to the student and parent population asking what holidays they celebrate at home and might like to see included in school activities.

15. At Rolling Hills Elementary, there is a large segment of the student body who misses school to celebrate an event on the same day every year. This trend has proved to be ongoing and consistent.

    What can be done to encourage these students cease missing school for the same day every year?

    (A) Seek feedback from the teacher and student/parent population about educational ways to honor the day while school is in session.

    (B) Send out a newsletter reminding parents of the importance of students attending every school day they are physically able.

    (C) Close the school each year on the anticipated day.

    (D) Celebrate every holiday that falls on a school day.

16. Students at Marshall Primary School rush through their lunches to make it out to recess quickly. While the school is academically in good standing, the social elements still have room for growth. Even though the school has a diverse student population, it always appears to be that the same groups of students are sitting together at lunch and playing together at recess.

    What would be effective at encouraging students to interact outside their close circle of friends more?

    (A) Participate in nationwide opportunities such as "Mix It Up Day" and similar events that encourage students to mingle with a new crowd.

    (B) Make lunchtime longer.

    (C) Start having assigned seats.

    (D) Switch recess to be before the lunch break.

17. At Young Elementary School, students often get dropped off on school grounds up to an hour before the first bell rings. For the most part these students manage ok without supervision, but occasionally they get pretty rowdy and the weather is sometimes miserable for them.

    What can be done to ease this situation?

    (A) Send automated calls and texts to remind the parents about school in session hours.

    (B) Broadcast music outside from the time the first student arrives until the first bell rings.

    (C) Explore the possibility of opening up the cafeteria or gym early with teachers taking on a few morning supervision shifts per month.

    (D) Mail letters outlining local babysitting, nanny, and local before school care options.

18. A year-long exchange student at Buena Heights Charter School celebrates April Fools' Day by sticking a paper fish onto students' backs. The principal receives many student complaints about the practice throughout the day.

    What can be done to improve the situation?

(A) Call the student into the office and tell them to stop it immediately.
(B) Tell the complaining students to relax and lighten up.
(C) Advise the students to each play a practical joke on the exchange student, in the spirit of American tradition.
(D) Research and learn more about the traditions and practices of exchange students, and in the future share the details with the student body and staff so they know what to expect.

19. The test scores from the last testing cycle indicate that more than half of the students score below the state benchmark for science.
    What would effectively address this situation?

    (A) Have teachers redesign their lesson plans to include science instruction every day.
    (B) Form an after-school science club run by volunteers or grant-funded instructors, emphasizing practical applications of and fun ways to use science.
    (C) Start a campaign with posters, banners, and mailing boasting the logo, "Science Is Super."
    (D) Encourage students to begin using any hot and cold lunch leftovers for science experiments.

20. The parent of a gifted student notifies the principal that their gifted child is not being challenged in math. Even when the student has directly asked to have hard math, the teacher just hands out duplicates of the same in class math worksheet to complete.
    What can be done to better this situation?

    (A) Discuss the matter with the teacher.
    (B) Explore the possibility the student may have been misidentified as gifted.
    (C) Consult the gifted education standards to determine if duplicate worksheets are in alignment. Review standard with teacher and outline a satisfactory approach.
    (D) Bring it up at the next after-school staff meeting. Then ask the more seasoned teachers to provide advice on the matter.

21. Every day at 10 am the students who are working to overcome learning obstacles join a special session held in the cafeteria. During this time the students focus on the academic elements they find most difficult to master. PE is also held at 10 am two days a week for first-grade students. Some parents of first-graders expressed their displeasure with their students missing PE.
    What is the most effective solution?

    (A) Alleviate the parents' worries by explaining how PE is not as important as the learning their students are doing at the same time.
    (B) Acknowledge the concern, review the issue with involved staff, and then explore the possibility of the first-graders joining PE with a different grade class.
    (C) Switch the lesson times.
    (D) Direct the academic-focused class to relocate to the gym, so the first-grade students can do both simultaneously.

22. After receiving the standardized test scores in the mail last spring, 65 percent of the parents decided to opt their student out of participating in state testing.
    What will improve the rate of participation?

    (A) Send weekly reminders home about the importance of the testing for student education and the future of the school they attend.
    (B) At drop-off, express doubt to parting parents about the high number of families claiming suddenly to have a valid reason to opt out when last year they had none.
    (C) Start an after-school test-taking club to make it more fun and enjoyable.
    (D) Invite parents to share their concerns through surveys and school meetings. Review and address the issue most frequently brought up.

23. Ms. Finkelstein, a sixth-grade teacher, has brought to the principal a flyer that one of her students, Malcolm, has asked to give to all of his classmates. It is a flyer for a weekend athletic camp sponsored by his mosque as he and his family are practicing Muslims. The teacher questions whether it would be appropriate for her to allow these to be passed out as the remainder of her class are Christians and if the parents of these students would be upset.
    Which of the following is the best option for the principal?

    (A) Inform the student that he cannot pass these flyers out as they are religious in nature and therefore are not permitted.
    (B) Direct the teacher to send a note home to the parents of all the children to see if they would like to have the flyers and send flyers to those who reply.
    (C) Inform the student that the flyers must be redone and the mosque must be removed as the sponsor before they can be distributed.
    (D) Distribute the flyers as is and the parents will have to decide individually if they want to send their children.

24. The school counselor at Hartford Elementary School has a mini-fridge close by that is always stocked with string cheese. One of the kindergarteners stops by most mornings to chat and eat a snack.
    How should this be handled?

    (A) Interview the counselor and staff to determine if the child may qualify for services they are not currently receiving.
    (B) Stop the student in the hallway before entering the counseling office and advise them to head straight to class. Perform this task daily until the behavior is extinguished.
    (C) Ask the counselor to document each time a string cheese is distributed in order to bill the family accordingly.
    (D) Do not intervene.

25. Newly assigned teachers at Bagby Elementary School are not often making it through their first two years of teaching before resigning their position.
    What could be done to improve this?

    (A) Provide better coffee in the teachers' lounge.

(B) Establish a mentor program, where experienced teachers meet with those just entering the field for advice and support.

(C) Initiate weekly new teacher support group lunches, where the newest additions come together to share stories and seek support.

(D) Offer more opportunities for professional development and growth.

26. At Lakeview High School a weekend tragedy lead to the death of a young and vibrant student. Within days, the principal is presented with a signed petition that has been circulating around the school and demands to erect a fountain and statue in memory of the departed classmate.
     How could this most effectively be handled?

(A) Start fundraising, statues are not inexpensive.

(B) Ask if a student representative has been in touch with the family for consent.

(C) Guide the project so as to remember the student by which is less prominent and permanent.

(D) Encourage the students to raise money to gift to the family.

27. Every year during the first week of school at Dooneyway Elementary, it is painfully obvious which students are new to the school. These are the students who eat lunch alone and stand alone at recess.
     What could improve this occurrence?

(A) Develop a new school motto that incorporates being a warm, welcoming place.

(B) Before each school year ends, have students vote for ambassadors for their grade who will lead the welcoming and inclusion of any new students in the fall.

(C) Have a staff member introduce the newest students and walk them around for a tour of the grounds.

(D) Assign the new students a buddy to shadow all day.

28. As is often the case in lower grades, the principal at Flourtown Primary School has many students being sent to the office for physical altercations with peers.
     What may lower this occurrence and prevent recurrence?

(A) More parent volunteers on playground duty.

(B) Shorter recesses.

(C) School announcements over the loudspeaker in the mornings reminding everyone to be kind and caring.

(D) Incorporate a conflict wheel or similar concept that displays options for how to deal with conflict before it escalates into a physical expression.

29. After the Fall Dance at Lincoln Middle School, it became apparent that the school needed to lead its students toward kindness. Before launching the campaign of kindness, the principal must select a method to determine the effectiveness of the movement.
     What would be effective at measuring change in perception or awareness about kindness?

(A) Ask the students after end of campaign if they think they changed.

(B) Have teachers observe and informally keep track of overall level of kindness before and after the campaign.

(C) Ask parents to report changes they have noticed at the end of the campaign.

(D) Distribute anonymous surveys before the campaign begins and again at the end to collect self-report details on understanding and valuing kindness.

30. At Huffstra High School, the teachers have all been set up with accounts to use Google classroom to augment their in-class teaching and to share assignments without using paper. So far, use of this tool has been somewhere between slow to stalled.

What might improve the use?

(A) Send one teacher to training on the products and then have them return to conduct one-on-one training with remaining staff.

(B) Direct teachers to use their next professional development day to complete some self-paced online training by watching videos and reading tutorials.

(C) Do not push the issue, they will dig in when they are ready.

(D) Have a kickoff event to inform and engage the intended users, followed by a campaign of weekly how to's, practical applications, and ongoing use support.

31. Recently some parents at Yuka Middle School complained about music that was being played during free time in PE; they claimed the references were adult in nature and not age appropriate for the student body.

How should this be remedied?

(A) Advise the teacher to contact their representative.

(B) Review teacher guidelines, and discuss and monitor for compliance.

(C) Report the details to a local media outlet.

(D) Inform the teacher not to play music in class again.

32. At Jensen Elementary School, the PTA provides teachers a fair allotment each year to use for field trips. One teacher has yet to use their field trip funds.

What is an appropriate step for a principal to take in this case?

(A) Discuss with the teacher obstacles or objections they are experiencing.

(B) Hold a conference with the teacher and remind them to get planning a trip ASAP.

(C) Request a different teacher and simply invite them along on a trip.

(D) Just let it slide, there will be more funds for classes that want to use them.

33. Jefferson High School is a place where a dedicated team of teachers can often be found working past dinnertime many nights a week.

How can a new principal show that they carry the same ethic?

(A) Be flexible enough to let teachers guide the direction of the school.

(B) Make sure the teachers know how easy they are to get along with.

(C) Occasionally order pizza for the late-night cohort.

(D) Act on any suggestion from the teacher impropriety swiftly and according to guidelines firmly.

34. A large number of parents called and came by the Tandy Elementary School principal office after their students participated in a dissection project without consent or a chance to opt out.

    How should this be handled?

    (A) Hold a conference to review standards and best practices with the teacher involved.
    (B) Schedule a slot to discuss the topic on public radio.
    (C) Have a conference, inviting all the parents and the teacher involved.
    (D) Review standards with all the teachers at the next professional day.

35. The assistant principal at Tide Elementary has heard murmurs that the professional development and continuing ed seminars that some of the teachers and staff are attending are short on content and a breeze to complete.

    What should the assistant principal do in this case?

    (A) Call all involved teachers into a meeting where they are warned to be extra careful not to make any mistake.
    (B) Do some calling around and see if anyone else has heard about this.
    (C) Inform the principal and reach out to the accrediting agency of the credit-offering institution.
    (D) Do nothing, it is likely just a rumor.

36. Every year during the last weekend of June, there is a nonschool-related event; many local principals and assistant principals gather to celebrate the changing seasons and blow off a little end-of-the-year steam. While attendance is optional and the event is in no way supported by the district, it had become a favorite tradition for many school leaders over the years. During the last event, one of the assistant principals in attendance made some unpleasant jokes; most of the people within earshot abruptly walked away.

    What is an effective way to proceed in this situation?

    (A) Take no action other than distancing yourself from that individual.
    (B) Contact the principal and inform of the unsavory situation.
    (C) Reach out to the head of the PTA at the offender's school to inform of what happened.
    (D) Start asking around to see if anyone knows if this is an ongoing occurrence.

37. Since accepting a position at a school in a different town, a former colleague of Principal Jordan's has been great about staying in touch. In fact, there are e-mails arriving in the inboxes of all teachers and staff at Principal Jordan's school. While harmless in nature, they lack useful content, and are often sent to dozens of recipients at a time.

    How should this be addressed?

    (A) Mark the sender as a sender of SPAM and block all future correspondence.
    (B) Ask teachers and staff not to respond to the e-mails in hopes that they will dwindle without further encouragement.

(C) Accept the attempt to maintain a friendly connection graciously.

(D) Reach out to the individual and ask them directly to stop inundating your inboxes unless it is school related.

38. At Jackstown Middle School, the principal is usually the last one to arrive before the doors open to students in the morning.

Is this of consequence to the teachers or students?

(A) Yes, it makes the principal unavailable for teachers or parents to approach before the start of the day.

(B) Yes, it makes it harder to get a decent parking spot.

(C) No, as long as the principal makes it before the start of a school day, it is no big deal.

(D) No, being available before the start of a school day is the least important part of a principal's day.

39. A growing number of parents are reaching out to the principal at Reeds Tuft High School because they are not getting responses to their inquiries from a lit teacher. The principal is informed that the teacher is slow or never responds to e-mails and phone call questions.

What should the next steps be?

(A) Assure the parents the situation will be improved shortly.

(B) Provide alternate contact details to reach the teacher.

(C) Direct parents to utilize other resources like Internet searching for information on lit topics.

(D) Review policy with teacher and perform subsequent monitoring for compliance.

40. After switching to a fifth-grade position, a long-time former second-grade teacher was in for a shock upon reading the spring health, family, and life choices curriculum. There were words in the lessons the teacher had never said before, much less said in front of thirty 10-year-olds. The teacher brings these concerns to the principal.

How should the principal address this?

(A) Advise the teacher to start practicing in private.

(B) Meet with the teacher to discuss if the move to fifth grade was the right one.

(C) Set the teacher up with a mentor who has taught the curriculum in the past.

(D) Direct the teacher to find a continuing ed class on the matter before springtime.

41. Part of the new Green Team's initiative is to get all staff and faculty to start parking one block away and walking from there. However, there is a lovely spot close to the building reserved for the principal.

What is the best way to proceed?

(A) Appeal to the Green Team to consider other measures.

(B) Park one block away and walk.

(C) Keep on parking in the reserved spot.

(D) Offer the head of the Green Team their own parking spot close to the building.

42. At Woodland Elementary most of the surrounding houses are adorned with fruit and nut tree farms.
    What is the best way to incorporate the surroundings in the curriculum?

    (A) Circulate petition to save the trees.
    (B) With permission from homeowners, carefully visit the trees as appropriate for curriculum; in return offer to pick ripe fruit for tree owners.
    (C) Watch the trees from the window.
    (D) Offer for students to rake fallen leaves.

43. There is an area where graffiti is an ongoing situation.
    What can be done to handle it?

    (A) Seek paint donations and student help to paint over as soon as possible after it arises.
    (B) Organize patrols to canvas the neighborhood for loiterers.
    (C) Put up "no graffiti here" signs.
    (D) Upon first discovering, notify the affected homeowners.

44. There is a community garden just eight houses away from a poverty-affected middle school.
    How can the proximity be leveraged to benefit the student population?

    (A) Encourage teachers to take their students to tour the space.
    (B) Allow students to visit the market stand at the community garden during the lunch break, in order to acquire healthy lunch choices.
    (C) Have students refrain from visiting the space to ensure students do not go wandering off.
    (D) Develop a plan to collaborate with the garden to set up a program of student garden work in exchange for gardening guidance, seeds, and produce.

45. The recently formed theater group at Charmington High School is in need of a space to perform their play.
    How might they engage in a partnership with the community to solve the situation?

    (A) Negotiate borrowing space in exchange for advertising space in the program, for trash pickup, or for some other service which might benefit the venue.
    (B) Simply perform outdoors at the high school open air theater.
    (C) Try to arrange borrowing a theater at a school 20 minutes away.
    (D) Film the performance and put it online; live theater is a dying art anyway.

46. There has been significant public outcry recently regarding the modernization of the neighborhood that Kellogg Elementary School is in. Town Hall meetings demand connections to a more historic time in the area.
    Is there a way the school could serve this cause?

    (A) Invite the parent population to attend and be vocal in town hall meetings.
    (B) Add to school newsletter tidbits on the matters of modernization to inform the community.

(C) Voice support for the neighborhood movement through media outlets.

(D) Enlist the help of volunteer students to paint a historic-themed mural on a neighborhood building.

47. The students at St Johns K-8 School do not have an art program. When a teacher chooses to incorporate it, occasionally students have the opportunity to complete some watercolor paintings and pencil sketches in class as part of the standard curriculum. There is no art-based curriculum or chances to explore more than the most basic art mediums.

    What is an effective way to get more art-based curriculum?

    (A) Instruct each classroom to turn on Bob Ross painting reruns after lunch recess each day.
    (B) Display prints of famous paintings in the hallways.
    (C) No need to intervene as those truly interested in art will seek it out on their own.
    (D) Recruit parent volunteers to develop a parent/community member lead art program even though the classes convene only infrequently.

48. A new principal to Gregory Heights Charter School is charged with improving student morale, as the culture of lackluster academics has been present for quite some time and is reflected in the attitudes of the school community.

    What might be a fast way to engage the school community?

    (A) In a newsletter and in the hallways, find opportunities to highlight some student and teacher achievements in the community.
    (B) Declare a pet day, where all students can bring in a pet for the day.
    (C) Hold a lottery where the luck winner can choose a new name for the school.
    (D) Once a month, invite the student with the highest grades to shadow the principal as a reward.

49. At a very small K–8 school that a new principle recently took over, there are no electives offered for the middle school students since the low enrolment prevents funding elective teaching positions. Up until now, in place of electives the students have independent study.

    What is an effective way to implement offering electives?

    (A) Let the middle school students help out in the classrooms of the younger grades; spending time with kids is like a free period anyway.
    (B) Start showing 80s movies and call it Film Studies elective.
    (C) Assign students to help out on the cafeteria and call it Intro to Cooking elective.
    (D) Make a request to parents and community members to donate time and supplies; then design available electives around the resources that are uncovered.

50. School day morning is always a busy time around Beatown Elementary School. It is not uncommon for parents to wait in line in their car for up to 10 minutes before reaching the most desirable student drop-off location. Crowds of cars form a continuous line of spewing fumes where young lungs are entering the school.

What can be done to improve this situation?

(A) Designate a three-block perimeter around the school that is a vehicle-free zone.

(B) Post sign asking drivers to shut off their engines while waiting in drop-off line.

(C) Make Tuesdays and Thursdays "park and walk to school" days.

(D) Designate an idle-free perimeter around the school, with drop-offs taking place at the edge of the perimeter.

51. Park Elementary School is nestled among old growth evergreens and is a favorite destination of dog owners from all around the area. The dog owners almost always wait until school is out for the day before bringing their dogs to play in the open green space. Despite the many signs posted around the perimeter of the school, they consistently let their dogs off leash and do not clean up after their pets. This causes risk to the students who play after school and also makes for some very unsanitary conditions for students the next day.

What is an effective approach to handle this situation?

(A) Nothing can be done; it is after-school hours.

(B) Bring a dog whistle in an attempt to annoy and deter the dogs from playing there.

(C) Report the high number of off-leash dogs and noncleaning owners to local animal control authorities.

(D) Use a megaphone to broadcast the rules clearly to the afterhours school grounds users.

52. At Kingley Elementary students are motivated to help a cause they are passionate about, but are unsure how to proceed.

What might the principal suggest as a way to raise funds and awareness?

(A) Take out an ad in the local newspaper.

(B) Hold school assemblies on the topic.

(C) Reach out to other schools for advice.

(D) Allow the students to hold a coin drive to collect funds for the purpose of donating.

53. Gadsden Science and Technology Magnet School has embraced and accepted electronic communication between students, parents, teachers, and administration. Each student is assigned an e-mail account and all parents are encouraged to communicate electronically with faculty and staff. The technology lab assistant discovered an open chat log between two students who failed to log out of their respective accounts on the school computers. She is disturbed because the chat log contains sexually provocative language as well as profanity-laced exchanges between the two students and threats against some faculty. All students signed an Acceptable Use Agreement, which prohibits such behavior and spells out sanctions, so she prints the log out and takes it to the assistant principal. The two students are located and facing possible suspension. The parents are irate as they saw this as a blatant violation of the

student's privacy rights as this was a good-natured albeit racy conversation between two adolescents.

What is the best course of action for the assistant principal as it relates to dealing with the behavior?

(A) Uphold the suspension, the Acceptable Use policy prohibits the behavior and the student should have no expectation of privacy as this is a computer and Internet access is owned and operated by the school and school district.

(B) This is an obvious violation of student privacy and the suspension should be avoided. The students had a reasonable expectation of privacy when they signed up for the school e-mail accounts.

(C) Uphold the suspension but limit the punishment to violations relating to the use of vulgar language and sexually provocative language. It is clear they did not mean to harm the faculty as the threats were not carried out.

(D) Do not suspend or punish the students. Suspend their computer privileges and help the students understand they should use better language on the Internet.

54. The principal of Hackney High School (HHS) recently received a new budget allocation from the superintendent of schools, which drastically reduces spending for the upcoming school year. The local school board has approved a reduction in force (RIF) due to a budgetary crisis and has directed the superintendent to oversee district-wide cuts in personnel. HHS received over 12 percent less than last year, and their RIF plan requires three full-time employees (FTE) within certified ranks and two FTE within classified staff. In addition, the school must make significant gains in student achievement (standardized test scores) or face corrective action from the district and state agencies. The faculty and staff have heard about the RIF and have become somewhat alarmed that it will be used to get rid of teachers and staff who have disagreed with the principal and district administration.

What is the best strategy to solicit input and support from faculty and staff, while also insuring necessary academic strategies to improve student test scores?

(A) The principal should develop a seniority chart that lists those teachers with the least amount of experience and submit those names to the superintendent for possible RIF action.

(B) The principal should work collaboratively with his faculty, staff, parents, and other stakeholders to develop a plan to improve student test scores balanced with available resources.

(C) The principal should develop a chart of teachers who have consistently produced the highest test scores ranging down to those teachers who have had the lowest level of productivity. Those with the least amount of productivity should be submitted for RIF.

(D) The principal should develop an academic improvement plan to improve student achievement and allow the superintendent to select the faculty and staff to be RIF.

55. All principals must insure that student records and information is kept in the strictest levels of confidentiality. Because students often speak with teachers as

well as guidance counselors when they have personal issues, they must all be trained to know when the contents of these contacts and records are protected by confidentiality rules.

Which of the following is a situation when confidentiality rules prohibit educators from sharing the contents of a student's conversation or records?

(A) When the student shares information that they will harm themselves.
(B) When the student shares that they intend to hurt someone else.
(C) When the information is requested for medical reasons.
(D) When an employer requests information for a hiring decision.

56. There are a few instances when a school is allowed to release student information that would otherwise be held due to restraints of confidentiality.

Which of the following is not a situation when student confidential information is allowed to be released by the school?

(A) A search warrant issued by a local or federal court.
(B) When student information is requested via a court-issued subpoena.
(C) When a parent makes a request to view their child's records.
(D) When a college requests additional information for an admission decision.

57. Schools and school divisions must develop policies and procedures for the maintenance of records. The principal of Morgan High school inherited a record room that has records that span the entire 157-year life of the school. The division superintendent has asked the school board attorney to aid the principal and school district in developing a policy that covers all of the areas of maintenance of student records.

All of the following areas must be included in the policy EXCEPT:

(A) Physical security for the records.
(B) Access to records.
(C) Format of the records to be kept.
(D) Destruction of records.

58. A parent has complained to the principal that she believes her child's teacher is making inappropriate contact with her child. The mother reports that her son is secretive and will not discuss the e-mails, text messages, and cellular phone calls that he receives from his math teacher. The principal has been asked to investigate and finds that the student and teacher have communicated constantly after school in what could be deemed inappropriate terms. To insure that this does not happen again, the principal is developing a policy on electronic communication with students.

Which of the following is not essential or appropriate for the electronic communication policy?

(A) Do not e-mail student for personal reasons.
(B) Do not leave telephone messages for students on the family home phone.
(C) Eliminate text messages as a form of communication, except in emergency.
(D) Avoid communication on social networks.

59. An irate parent complained to the principal that a teacher had sent an inappropriate electronic message to her work site. The parent produced a copy of the e-mail, which included her student's failing grades and multiple class absences that had led to his nine-week grade of 24 percent. The parent sent an e-mail back to the teacher asking that the teacher refrain from sending messages like this to her work site as it was both embarrassing and frustrating as all electronic messages are warehoused on a server at her company. The principal found that the web address was given by the parent.

What policy change would alleviate this and future other possible issues with electronic communication with parents?

   (A) Ask teachers to respond to complex messages from parents by telephone or face to face rather than electronic message.
   (B) Send only paper messages home to the parents and do not send electronic communications.
   (C) Post all information about student grades and other information on the school website for parents to access.
   (D) Insure parents sign an electronic communication agreement that tells on which phone numbers and e-mail addresses they will receive school information.

60. Ms. Johnson comes to the principal and asks to speak about a conversation that she just had with a student. The principal is then told that the teacher called a student into the classroom to talk with him after she noticed that he had a large bruise on the side of his neck. When she questioned him, he told her that he had gotten the injury skateboarding at the park, but she suspected it was the result of child abuse by his father. When she questioned him further, the student did admit that he got it in a fight. The teacher told the principal she was not certain it was the father and did not want to cause any unnecessary agitation or embarrassment to the family of the student.

Which of these is the most appropriate step for the principal to take?

   (A) Since the child did not admit it was the parent who struck him, leave it alone until he has concrete proof.
   (B) Begin an investigation by contacting the mother to see if she would admit it was the father who injured the student.
   (C) Immediately get the student and take him to the local police station to press assault charges against his father.
   (D) Immediately report the suspected child abuse issue to the local child protective service office and let them launch an investigation.

61. The principal of Gaston High school has been directed to either generate more revenue or face deep cuts in the school's athletic budget. One proposal that has been placed in consideration by the Advisory Board is to require all students to pay a participation fee if they want to participate in junior varsity or varsity sports. The fee would be determined by the overall operating cost for the sport. A parent group has begun to protest the decision saying that it will keep poor students away because they will not be able to afford the mandatory participation fees.

Which would be the most appropriate response to the parents' concerns?

(A) Inform the parents that these fees will keep all sports, so they need to be supported by everyone including parents.
(B) Agree with the parent group and do not implement the practice, which will lead to ending several of the team sports.
(C) Ask the parents to donate funds for the low-income students who cannot afford the participation fee and therefore guarantee sports survive.
(D) Ask the parents and other stakeholders to meet with the principal and develop a fair and equitable process that will replace this proposal.

62. The Conway School System recently received a federal grant that they have distributed to the local high schools to develop strategies to improve student achievement on standardized examination in math and science. Each principal has been charged with developing a plan for the funds that will improve test scores.

Which of the following options is the best strategy to develop a plan that will improve student achievement?

(A) The principal should look at current educational research on strategies and implement the one that has had the most success in a similar setting.
(B) The principal should look at other school districts that have similar school populations and scores and select the most successful one to implement.
(C) The principal should convene a committee of stakeholders to identify the strategies that would lead to most improvement in student achievement.
(D) The principal should initiate strategies to improve student achievement based upon his own professional experiences.

63. Ms. Smith, the art teacher, asked students to draw a picture of the person most influential in their lives and to write a one-page essay on how that person has influenced their lives. Students were to present the portraits and the essay in class on that week. Adam Spencer drew a picture of a bearded man with the caption: Jesus Christ—the most influential person in my life. He then proceeded to read his essay about his religious conversion to Christianity and the role of Jesus Christ. Ms. Smith interrupted him and asked him to meet her in the hallway. She informed him that he could not read his essay as it contained religious material and she had meant an actual person he had met. Adam was upset and contacted his mother, who contacted the principal to ask him to intercede. She argued Adam had the right to choose Jesus Christ and Ms. Smith was wrong.

Which of the following responses is the best legal response to this situation?

(A) Inform Ms. Spencer that religious convictions could not be spoken in class and Adam had not completed the assignment as directed by Ms. Smith—deny her request.
(B) Allow Adam to make the presentation—insure that the presentation is about why Jesus Christ is the most influential person in his life and does not seek to influence others.
(C) Allow Adam to make his presentation but not in the presence of the students—only in front of Ms. Smith.

(D) Inform Ms. Spencer that Adam would have to redo the assignment and make a presentation that is not religious in nature.

64. Mr. Strong is the AP World History Teacher and part of the curriculum includes conflicts between Christians and Muslims, including the Crusades and recent Middle East conflicts that have pitted these religious following against each other. The textbooks and state-approved supplementary materials contain literature that speaks negatively about the Muslims and other followers of Islam. Two students in the class are practicing Muslims and the class content conflicts with the teaching they receive in their homes and mosques. The information will be part of the Advanced Placement examination and is part of the state curriculum. The parents of the two Muslim students have protested that their children are being fed negative information about their religion and people and ask the principal to intercede.

    Which of the following would be the most appropriate response to this dilemma?

    (A) Inform the Muslim parents that this is state-approved content and that the students can be moved to another class that does not deal with this issue.
    (B) Inform Mr. Strong that he is to teach both the state-approved curriculum and include information provided by the children's parents as well.
    (C) Allow the students to excuse themselves from the class when this section of the coursework is being taught and not grade it on their AP exam.
    (D) Inform the parents that this is state-approved curriculum, and while they may find it objectionable, it is required information they need to know but not embrace.

65. At Hartsville High School, a student, Carla, prays audibly before eating her meal during the lunch period. A couple of students begin to join her. Several other students begin to sit at the same table during their lunch schedule to be able to join her. Over the next week, several more students ask for a schedule change so they can sit at the "Christian table" during lunch and engage in this practice each day. The parents support the schedule changes and contact the assistant principal and principal to ask for the changes stating they would not affect their students' academic schedules. The assistant principal refuses the requests. Carla's mother and several other parents call to complain and insist on coming to school each day during lunch time to make sure the students' rights are protected. That same week, another mother calls to complain that children were pressuring her child, an atheist, to sit at the "Christian table" and pray with them.

    Which of the following would be the best (legal) response to these requests?

    (A) Immediately end the practice of students praying "out loud" at the lunch tables and instruct them to pray individually and not in groups.
    (B) Allow the schedule requests as well as schedule change requests from students who feel uncomfortable during the practice to protect all students' rights.
    (C) Set aside a separate area of the cafeteria for the praying students so they can pray out loud and not bother other students.

(D) Allow students to continue the practice during both lunch periods as long as it is voluntary and does not coerce or bother other students.

66. The normal practice for high school commencement exercise is that the valedictorian is given the opportunity to speak to his fellow graduating classmates. Each student who earns this honor must submit their speech to the senior sponsor who reads it and submits it to the principal for approval. This year's valedictorian Matthew Robinson has prepared his address and submitted it to the senior sponsor, who has in turn submitted it to the principal. The address includes several biblical scriptures and references to religion including thanking God for his many blessings and mercy. It also includes reference to the recent school board election that supported a conservative agenda and has softened its stance on prayer and religion in schools. His speech ends with a long New Testament Bible verse.
    Which of the following would best deal with this situation?

    (A) Leave the speech as it is—it is the student's constitutional right to pray and use biblical scriptures.
    (B) Help the student to rewrite the speech and insure that it does not have any references to the Bible or other religious information.
    (C) Replace the student with a replacement student speaker who does not have a speech with those references to the Bible and religion.
    (D) Inform the student that he would have to remove the biblical reference and scriptures or not be allowed to speak.

67. At Swift Creek Middle School, a group of sixth-graders drafted and dropped off a letter to the principal stating their dissatisfaction with the solar system curriculum units. The letter complained that while the students just finished an in-depth unit on the solar system last week in science, they are now beginning a math unit revolving around the same content. They are bored by the lack of variety and want something different.
    What is an effective approach to addressing these concerns?

    (A) Enlisting the help of teachers, review lesson plans and then develop and implement a timeline that allows for a cohesive unit on the solar system across subjects.
    (B) Suggest that the students seek variety in their music and their friends, and to accept school as it is already fine.
    (C) Reserve all topics relating to space to be taught solely by the science teacher.
    (D) Declare the theme of the year to be the Solar System.

68. A group of students have approached the principal about using the multipurpose room for a student-led prayer and Bible study session each week. They have submitted the necessary paperwork, and the study group meeting will take place either before class or after school on a weekly basis. From time to time a few faculty members will come and join them in prayer and study. The principal approved the request for the students to use the room, but a local atheist group has started to complain that the school is sponsoring prayer, which is in violation

of state and federal laws, and that the adult teachers by their presence are in fact leading the prayer—another violation.

Which of the following is the best legal response to these accusations?

(A) Ask the teachers to remove themselves from the student-led sessions as this has led to a violation of state and federal laws on prayer in schools.
(B) Find another location off-campus for the students to hold these sessions and provide transportation if needed.
(C) Request the students to have the sessions on the weekends when school is not in session.
(D) The current practices are all permissible under state and federal laws—take no action.

69. The Supreme Court has set precedent and affirmed a number of cases that deal with how religion can be approached and even taught in our public schools. There are basic principles that all public schools must adhere to when religion is included in their curriculum and part of the school day.

Which of the following is not an acceptable standard for public schools?

(A) The school's approach to religion is academic, not devotional.
(B) The school strives for student awareness of religions, but does not press for student acceptance of any religion.
(C) The school may expose students to a diversity of religious views, but may not impose any particular view.
(D) The school sponsors the practice of religion, not the study of religion.

70. Two students were brought to the office after engaging in a physical altercation by the physical education teacher. One of the students is Hector, a Hispanic student who has had some difficulty in his classes due to his limited language proficiency. He speaks broken English and is often picked on by some of the students. Upon investigation, the assistant principal found that John pushed Hector in the back and was obviously the aggressor in the fight. Hector took offense with the push and then struck back at John and the fight ensued. The school district has a policy that when two students engage in a fight, both will be suspended for ten days out of school, regardless of who was the aggressor. The parents of Hector appealed the decision to the principal and superintendent, stating that they or Hector did know about the policy because of their inability to read and comprehend English.

Which of these is the best option for the principal?

(A) Uphold the suspension—it is the responsibility of the parents to insure that their child knows all of the rules and follows them.
(B) Grant the appeal and insure that a copy of the disciplinary rules and procedures is made available to all English language learner families and students.
(C) Allow Hector to spend his suspension in the In-school Detention Center rather that out of school.
(D) Issue Hector a suspension—but one that is shorter than the one for John as he did not know the policy but is guilty nonetheless.

71. The football coach of Langston High school came into the locker room and quietly notified the players who had been randomly selected for drug testing to come to the training room to give a sample to the representative from Omega Services. Omega Services had the contract with the school district to complete drug testing for employees, student-athletes, and other personnel. Ten players were selected and all ten submitted a sample, but results came back for everyone except Athlete #29. The student was told by the coach to submit another sample, but he refused to offer the second sample saying that it violated his rights. The coach informed the student that he was therefore suspended from the team and may face a year-long suspension from athletics for noncompliance. The parents of the student protested and appealed to the principal and superintendent.

    Which of the following options would best adhere to the policy and protect the student's rights?

    (A) Instruct the student to give the urine sample as directed or face the penalty. His giving another sample does not violate the policy.
    (B) Allow the student to give a urine sample to his own doctor so that it will be more carefully monitored and the results will be sent to the school.
    (C) Suspend him immediately as his refusal to give a sample is proof that he is abusing drugs.
    (D) Allow the student to participate without giving a urine sample and verifying that he is drug free. He should not be punished for their error.

72. Justin King was an eleventh-grader at Madison High School who was anonymously publishing a nonapproved newspaper called *CHAOS* and was distributing the newspaper during and after school hours. King had written a series of articles that he said would "disrupt the school day and help students escape the repressive regime that stifles student creativity." King often printed activities that students could do that would cause administration to spend time fixing problems and less time supervising students. His activities included clogging bathroom sinks, opening alarmed fire doors, and even a list of directions on how students could hack school computers. After an investigation, he was later discovered and admitted to printing the paper that was wildly popular. For his promotion of these subversive and disruptive activities he was suspended and faced possible expulsion. He and his parents appealed the suspension and stated he did not actively engage in any of the activities and his rights to these articles were protected under the constitution as free speech.

    Which of the following option is the best strategy for the principal when faced with the appeal?

    (A) Uphold the suspension—but not the expulsion as there is no proof he participated in the disruptive activities, just promoted them.
    (B) Grant the appeal—allow him to return as he did not physically commit the acts.
    (C) Grant the appeal—but only if he agrees to shut down the website, pay damages, and apologize to the school.
    (D) Uphold the suspension and expulsion recommendation—he actively endorsed, supported, and directed the disruptive activities.

73. Mark Johnson is a senior at Leavenworth High School and he created a website that asked for comments that were critical of the school administration and some teachers. The website allows his fellow students to post comments as well as pictures taken illegally with cell phone cameras of teachers and administrators. Some of the comments are profanity laced and many offer very negative comments about the personal lives of administrators. One of the students posted a comment that stated "Miller (assistant principal of LHS) should be killed" and several students offered comments in agreement. On Friday, a student was arrested for attempted murder of Mr. Miller as he fired several shots at Miller after a football game. The same student had posted a comment on Johnson's site declaring he would kill Miller. Johnson was taken in for questioning and immediately charged and later suspended from school with a recommendation for expulsion. His parents have appealed the suspension to the principal with notice to the school board.

    Which of the following is the best course of action for the principal?

    (A) Grant the appeal—the student could not be held responsible for the mental state of the student who attempted the murder; he was just running the site.
    (B) Grant the appeal—but if he is eventually charged with a crime, begin the proceeding to expel him from school.
    (C) Uphold the suspension—but if he is cleared of any criminal or civil charges, reinstate the expulsion proceedings.
    (D) Uphold the suspension—he created the site and personally endorsed and supported opportunity for disruptive actions to occur at the school.

74. An irate parent stood up at the Monroe Middle School parent-teacher association meeting and told the principal that her daughter has been bullied so much by some of her classmates that she refuses to come to school. Soon several other parents also spoke about some of the same challenges they have to get their children to school because they fear for their safety. They immediately asked the principal what she would do to end the offensive behavior that was harming so many students. The principal immediately organized a committee to develop strategies to combat bullying in their school.

    The committee found that effective programs include all of the following EXCEPT:

    (A) Increase supervision.
    (B) Begin when children are young.
    (C) Teach inclusion.
    (D) Teach children to take a stand by fighting back if accosted.

75. The media coordinator at Hofstra Middle School reported to the principal that several parents had come to the school media center and voiced their concern about several books that had references to homosexuality and atheism. They presented to the coordinator a list of books that they believed should be removed from the library and asked her to give it to the principal. All of the books had been approved by the local school board and the state department of education, but the parents have promised to boycott school functions if they are not removed.

Which of the following is the best response to this situation?

(A) Since the books are board and state approved, leave them in the media center and inform parents—they can give written approval for their students to read them.

(B) Do not remove them from the library—but rather move them to another part of the medical center that students cannot access without permission.

(C) Ask the parents to look over your entire list of books in the media center and they can then give a complete list of all the books they want removed.

(D) If the books are offensive to parents, just remove them and end the controversy.

76. The principal of Pontiac High school was summoned to the assistant principal's office who presented him an application for club sponsorship by the Gay Student Alliance. This would allow them the ability to use school classrooms and other facilities as other student clubs and organizations. The organization had a faculty sponsor, bylaws, and all of the other requirements to form a club at the high school. When the principal arrived back at the office, he was greeted by a group of parents, who had somehow learned of the club application and were there to express their disapproval. The principal then got a phone call from the district superintendent and a school board member who were also inquiring whether the principal would approve the application.

Which of the following options is the best strategy for the principal to take concerning the student club application?

(A) Deny the application—there is parental disapproval of such a club existing in the school.

(B) Deny the application—approving the application would give the perception that the school, principal, and school board are promoting homosexuality.

(C) Approve the application with conditions that they not publicly engage in homosexual activity.

(D) Approve the application—it meets all of the requirements for sponsorship and denial would possibly violate the students' civil rights.

77. Several parents of students with educational disability have voiced their concern that their children's academic needs are not being met. In their IEP meetings, they have told the Special Education Coordinator that their students lose so much of the information taught to them during the regular 180-day school year. They requested a mandatory summer session for special needs students so they can keep up, retain the information, and be ready for the next school year. The parents came as a group to the principal when the coordinator told them there was no enough money to fund the self-contained classrooms during the summer months for the nine children as that would mean employment of five certified special education teachers and four teacher assistants. A look at the students' records did show a measurable drop in achievement from the end of the year to the beginning of the next year.

Which of the following is the best strategy for the principal to take?

(A) Meet with the parents and inform them that although it may be needed, there is not enough money to fund a special education summer session.

(B) Meet with the parents and inform them that they can have the summer session, but they will have to pay a sum to fund payment of the faculty and staff.

(C) Meet with the parents and inform them that they may be able to get the services if they transferred their children to the neighboring affluent district.

(D) Meet with the parents and inform them that if the IEP committees agreed this was necessary, we would find a way to fund the summer sessions.

78. The principal has been alerted that two rival gangs had a major fight at the local mall and a substantial number of these gang members and their associates attend Mebane High School. The bus drivers have radioed in that there is a lot of chatter on their routes about the fight between the two community-based groups and the possibility that there might be trouble at school. After placing all faculty and staff on alert, two of the rival groups face off in the open area near the cafeteria. No punches are thrown, but the two identified leaders exchange threats. The two students leaders and their close associates are brought to the office and the principal makes the decision to remove (suspend) them from school.
    What is the appropriate legal justification for this step by the principal?

    (A) The principal knew that these students were trouble makers so he had the right to suspend them before they got in more trouble.

    (B) The principal did not have a legal justification to suspend the students and should return them to class.

    (C) The principal had the authority to suspend the schools as he believed that their presence there would lead an environment that was not safe for other students.

    (D) The principal should not suspend the students from school but rather send them to the alternative school to separate them from the population.

79. The security chief has found information that a student may have brought a weapon on campus but may have passed it on to another student. The principal decides to first bring in the student who he believes has the weapon; on searching him, his personal belonging, and his locker, he found no weapon. Five students who came to school with the student in his car are summoned to the office and all are asked to open their purses, book bags, and lockers for searches. All five comply with the request to search their book bags, but three of the five do not comply with the request to search their purses.
    What would be the best (legal) action for the principal to take?

    (A) Search the two students who complied and allow the other three to go back to class.

    (B) Because the three did not comply, it would not be fair to search the others— let them return to class.

    (C) Contact the parents of the students who refuse to comply and get to persuade them to do so.

    (D) Call in the school resource officer (deputy sheriff) and ask him to search the students' purses who did not comply.

80. Larkin Elementary has been identified by the state as a priority school designated for academic improvement. The school's principal, Mr. Byrd, consults with district administration, but Larkin is the first school in the district to receive such designation and the district appears to lack the necessary expertise. Learning that a neighboring school district previously dealt with a similar situation, Mr. Byrd obtains administration's approval to adopt the neighboring district's school improvement model, but opposition immediately surfaces when the elementary school staff and parents learn of the proposed plan. Explain how Mr. Byrd should proceed.
    What is the best course of action for the principal to take?

    (A) Schedule time to speak at the next board meeting in order to explain the reason for adopting a neighboring district's improvement plan.
    (B) Mail letters to parents explaining the need for school improvement.
    (C) Call a meeting with all building staff in order to announce how the plan will be implemented.
    (D) Contact the school district central offices for professional school improvement support, and begin the job of organizing a school improvement committee.

81. Soon after being hired as a new principal, you conduct a survey to determine the staffs' experience in working with new curriculum. To your dismay, you find that only a third of the staff have direct experience in teaching the new curriculum. Describe how you would implement a plan to develop the capacity of the staff.
    (A) Order curriculum material designed by a reputable curriculum development publisher for the staff to read prior to beginning the work of implementation.
    (B) Arrange curriculum training for select staff members, organize departments into groups, and develop a curriculum planning schedule.
    (C) Hire a group of outside curriculum consultants to implement the curriculum.
    (D) Appropriate and implement a curriculum from a neighboring school district.

82. An irate parent has telephoned the principal and complained that the guidance secretary has informed her that she will not make copies of her students' academic grades, transcripts, and disciplinary record unless the parent first comes to the school and pays 10 cents per copy for the nearly 40 pages she is requesting. She tells the principal that she knows her rights as a parent are being violated under the Family Educational Rights and Privacy Act (FERPA) and he needs to have the records copied and ready for her pickup when she arrives from her job in the next town, which is less than ten miles away. She has threatened a lawsuit and other actions if this is not done.
    What is the best (legal) action for the principal to take in this situation?

    (A) Direct the guidance secretary to allow the parent to see the records when she arrives and should she require copies—make them with payment in advance of 10 cents per page.
    (B) Direct the guidance secretary not to make the copies at all and proceed with her work.

(C) Direct the guidance secretary to make the copies and mail them to the parent at her legal address with a bill for the copies.

(D) Direct the guidance secretary to make the 40+ copies and deliver them to the office for pickup at no charge to the parent.

83. The PTA vice president suggested to the principal of Martin Middle School that the school offer some type of assistance or guidance to parents on how they can help their children improve their end-of-grade state test scores. A recent parent survey found that over 40 percent of respondents stated they did not know how to help other than to send their students to school each day. The principal asked the school guidance director to develop a plan to meet this need.

   Which of the following is the best strategy for the guidance director to take to assist parents to develop ways to help their child prepare for the test?

   (A) The guidance director should develop a system to provide support for parents including newsletters, e-mails, conferences, and other informational sessions.

   (B) The guidance director should send home a list of strategies for all parents to implement to help parents prepare their students for the upcoming test.

   (C) The best strategy is to concentrate on the students and instructional sessions as information sent home to student is normally not taken advantage of.

   (D) The guidance director should plan a test preparation session luncheon for parents so that they can share effective strategies.

84. Recent educational research has advocated principals become effective instructional leaders whose knowledge of effective instruction is matched by their attention to detail within their management style. One tool to help administrators meet these lofty goals is to master the walk-through technique.

   Which of the following is the biggest educational benefit of mastering an effective walk-through technique?

   (A) Walk-throughs are an excellent way for administrators to get exercise after sitting in the office all day.

   (B) Walk-throughs are an excellent opportunity for administrators to get into classrooms and create a rapport with students, maintain contact, and provide a basis for reflective learning environment.

   (C) Walk-throughs are an excellent opportunity to discover what teacher weaknesses are and record them for their formative and summative evaluation.

   (D) Walk-throughs are an excellent opportunity to see which teachers are strong and which are weak so that the strong teachers are assigned to the higher ability students.

85. Coach Sylvia Sanchez has been recently selected as the county's new athletic director. She is the first female to hold the position in a county that is dominated by several prolific male coaches who have won numerous state championships. The summer coaches' clinic and banquet will be held at James River High school and hosted by John Cortez, the school's principal and himself a former championship football coach. Martinez will be the keynote speaker for the event, but at the beginning of the meeting, she is met by uncooperative chatter and behavior by

these coaches who have outwardly expressed that a "woman cannot do this man's job." In addition, they are upset that one of their male coaching colleagues was not selected for the position.

Which of the following would be the best course of action for the hosting principal?

(A) Let her squirm—if she cannot take the heat, then she does not deserve to have the position and they are right to heckle her.
(B) As the host, call for a level of decorum that befits their professions—inform the coaches that they must respect the position if not its holder.
(C) Move quickly to her defense and take over the meeting. The coaches respect the male principal who is a former coach.
(D) Immediately step in and end the meeting. She is obviously not ready to lead the organization and this cannot happen in your school.

CONSTRUCTED-RESPONSE QUESTION TWO

In conducting classroom observations, a principal notes that most teachers in a high school rely heavily on lecture as a method of instruction. After consulting with the district's administration, including the professional development coordinator, the principal secures funding for a two-day workshop on cooperative learning. The workshop takes place and all the teachers are enthusiastic about it. In the next observations of faculty, two months after the interactive training, the school principal sees the same dependence on lecture as before.

What are the possible explanations from the perspective of curriculum, instruction, and assessment for what the principal sees?
What other ISLLC Standards can be integrated into your answer?

Appendix 2

Practice Test Two

1. D	30. D	59. D
2. C	31. B	60. D
3. B	32. A	61. D
4. C	33. D	62. C
5. D	34. A	63. B
6. A	35. C	64. D
7. B	36. A	65. D
8. A	37. D	66. D
9. D	38. A	67. A
10. A	39. D	68. D
11. D	40. C	69. D
12. D	41. B	70. B
13. B	42. B	71. A
14. D	43. A	72. D
15. A	44. D	73. D
16. A	45. A	74. D
17. C	46. D	75. A
18. D	47. D	76. D
19. B	48. A	77. D
20. C	49. D	78. C
21. B	50. D	79. D
22. D	51. C	80. D
23. D	52. D	81. B
24. A	53. A	82. A
25. B	54. B	83. A
26. C	55. D	84. B
27. B	56. D	85. B
28. D	57. C	
29. D	58. B	

Appendix 2

Practice Test Two

Answer Explanations

1. This question focuses on the ability to uncover deficiencies that may be preventing satisfactory student success. Responses (A), (B), and (C) do not consider the cause of decreasing enrolment. The correct response (D) will work to uncover undercurrents that are affecting student enrolment.—Standard 1

2. Responses (A) and (D) suggest that classroom management training is sufficient to contain disruptive episodes. Response (B) may prove to have opposite of the desired effect and will antagonize some students. The correct response (C) acknowledges the need for all learners to have a space that is behaviorally and academically appropriate.—Standard 1

3. This question focuses on access to high-quality education. Responses (A) and (C) provide little framework to encourage the pursuit of additional learning opportunities. (D) may provide some benefit, but is far from a comprehensive approach to improve the educational opportunities. (B) is the answer as this will provide insight into the best practices of leveled instruction.—Standard 1

4. The question focuses on the accessibility of academic success for all students. Since there is clearly either a lack of access or know-how, students must become acquainted and comfortable with the tools of technology, which is why (C) is the best answer. (A) does not offer any guidance or encouragement. Answers (B) and (D) do not provide any hands-on, applicable learning experiences to the students.—Standard 1

5. This question focuses on the success of each student. (A) and (C) are not the right response because they do not consider many involved stakeholders. (B) assumes that performance and behavior are a result of effort. The correct response is (D) because it includes seeking input from interested parties and crafting a specific plan.—Standard 1

6. This question focuses on the well-being of each student. (D) provides a specific resource to a large group, and while this will benefit the student, it is wasteful to provide a resource to so many students without a need. (B) and (C) suggest that no action be taken, which will result in no immediate improvement to the situation. (A) benefits the well-being of the student.—Standard 1

7. This question pertains to the ethics of school leadership. While it would be tempting to reveal the details to those whom it will have the most effect on, it is not an issue meant to be public. (A), (C), and (D) all include trying to inform chosen parent ahead of the rest. (B) is the appropriate answer.—Standard 2

8. This question focuses on acceptable behavior for those in a leadership position. (B) will not prove to be any help. (C) and (D) only temporarily mask the situation at hand but do nothing to resolve it. (A) is the answer as it includes directly addressing your concerns with the party involved.—Standard 2

9. This question focuses on professional standards that make a school environment a comfortable place for each student. (A) and (C) will only escalate the situation. (B) is a missed opportunity for parent and teacher growth. (D) allows the parents and teacher to use the experience as a platform with which to construct a positive alliance and cohesive team.—Standard 2

10. This question focuses on professional norms for school leaders. (B) and (C) do not take into account the flexibility that is necessary when interacting with a large sampling of the population. (D) assumes it is okay as long as no parent complains. (A) is the answer because it is possible that being playful might be an effective approach to connect with a high-needs or extremely shy student, but the majority of the time this type of greeting would not be acceptable.—Standard 2

11. This question focuses on decision making among school leaders. Even though the occurrence happened during a nonschool-related function, when there is a physical act of aggression, it should be reported promptly to the authorities regardless of who sponsored an event or when it is held, so (D) is the correct response. (A), (B), and (C) are not sufficient to investigate any physical threat the person may pose.—Standard 2

12. This question focuses on professional norms of schools leaders. (A) does not reflect any flexibility or school spirit. (B) and (C) expect the event to become an issue and may even invite it to become one. (D) is the answer because while it may be uncomfortable to participate, it is a limited engagement that will raise funds and provide some good entertainment to the school community.—Standard 2

13. (A) could make the students feel uncomfortable or singled out. (C) only focuses on diverse cultures for a limited amount of time. (D) suggests doing nothing at all. The correct response is (B), which allows the community to participate in cultural awareness and inclusion on an ongoing basis in the capacity with which they are comfortable.—Standard 3

14. (A) and (C) do nothing to further cultural growth or acceptance at the school. (B) may allow the event to become unmanageable or overrun with unapproved decorations. (D) is the correct answer because this allows every opinion to be considered and honored.—Standard 3

15. (B) does not reflect cultural awareness or sensitivity. (C) is a missed opportunity for student growth. (D) would prove overwhelming and impractical. (A) is the correct response because it incorporates ideas and input from a diverse population and is likely to result in harmless ways to acknowledge a variety of traditions.—Standard 3

16. This question focuses on the ability to respond to lacking cultural awareness within a school. (B) and (D) assume that longer break periods will lead to more

connections and new friendships, but students may still revert to their normal behaviors just for longer. (C) may lessen the enjoyment of the lunch break because the students lose some freedoms and the ability to connect with existing friends. (A) is the correct response because this provides students a gentle nudge to begin connecting with others outside their close circle of friends.—Standard 3

17. This question focuses on the ability to be culturally responsive in an effort to set up each student for success. (A), (B), and (D) do not aim to improve the situation or uncover why it exists. (C) is the correct response because it aims to offer shelter and supervision for all early-arriving students regardless of their ability to afford morning care options.—Standard 3

18. (A) and (B) are missed opportunities for growing awareness and understanding of a multitude of traditions. (C) is likely to make the exchange student feel singled out and ganged up on. (D) is the correct response because it allows the school community to grow their familiarity with and understanding of cultural norms other than their own.—Standard 3

19. This question focuses on the ability to develop academically rigorous curriculum. (A) is impractical and extremely time consuming. (C) relies on propaganda in place of providing more opportunities to learn. (D) would be messy and potentially unsafe. (B) provides the same opportunity to all students to improve their understanding of the subject through hands-on activities.—Standard 4

20. (A) and (D) do not take into consideration existing gifted instruction standards. (B) does not serve the academic well-being of the student. (C) allows for review and improvements and is the correct response.—Standard 4

21. This question focuses on providing an academically rigorous environment for each student. (A) may quiet the concern, but dissuades parents from realizing the value of physical fitness as part of a child's well-being. (C) would only be a solution for some of the students. (D) would prove to be a distraction and might overwhelm the students. (B) is the correct response because it is adaptive to fit the needs of all interested parties.—Standard 4

22. (A), (B), and (C) miss the opportunity for addressing the concerns of and partnering up with the parent population. (D) allows the concerns to be validated and sets the stage for movement in the right direction.—Standard 4

23. (D) is the best answer. If local school district policy or practice permits distribution or posting of noncurriculum-related materials on school grounds, the Free Speech Clause prevents a district from discriminating based on the viewpoints, including religious viewpoints, expressed in the materials. *Hedges v. Wauconda Cmty. Unit Sch. Dist. 118, 9 F.3d 1295 (7th Cir. 1993); Rivera v. East Otero Sch. Dist., 721 F. Supp. 1189 (D. Colo. 1989).* For example, when a district engaged in unconstitutional viewpoint discrimination refused to permit distribution of camp brochures expressing a religious viewpoint on otherwise permissible subject matter. *Hills v. Scottsdale Unified Sch. Dist. No. 48, 329 F.3d 1044 (9th Cir. 2003)* (per curium). Courts have held that schools do not violate the Establishment Clause by permitting religious viewpoints to be disseminated as part of an open forum for communication. For example, *Child Evangelism Fellowship of N.J. v. Stafford Twp. Sch. Dist., 233 F. Supp. 2d 647 (D.N.J. 2002)* (granting a preliminary injunction to give Christian youth group access to school's methods

of distributing nonschool materials to students and posting nonschool materials).
(B)—This is not the normal practice when advertisements from secular or Christian-based organizations sponsor event, so it is prohibited. (C) Removal of the Muslim references is discriminatory and biased and not permissible.—Standard 3

24. This question focuses on providing a caring place for students to learn. (B) and (C) may be interpreted as intimidating and do not serve to better the situation for the student. (D) would be a missed opportunity to provide additional care that may be needed. (A) is the informed choice that assists the student in connecting with a caring network of individuals.—Standard 5

25. (A) and (D) would likely only be short-term solutions. (C) would support the new teachers but is unlikely to provide them any additional tools to incorporate. (B) is the correct response because the new teachers can be supported, can connect with experienced professionals, and can learn from the years of classroom management.—Standard 5

26. (A) and (B) suggest that the project will move forward, but also sets the standard to erect a landmark every time a student passes away. (D) would benefit the family, but not allow the students the outlet they are seeking. (C) is the correct response because it allows the students to have a physical place to remember and honor the student, but in a way that is not disruptive.—Standard 5

27. This question focuses on leading an inclusive school community. (A) would be a nice addition, but unlikely to create new sentiment among the students. (C) would not help a new student connect with their peers. (D) restricts the new student to primarily interact with only one peer, and the peer could be reluctant to participate. (B) is the correct response because it relies on the students to elect their peers they deem most friendly and welcoming.—Standard 5

28. (A) and (B) may lower the occurrences on a short-term basis, but provide no plan for ongoing maintenance. (C) would set a good example, but might be forgotten about by recess time. (D) is the correct response because it incorporates actions that students can take for themselves to improve their situation and dissuade interactions from escalating into physical conflict. Visual reminders about the conflict resolution choices can be displayed around the playground.—Standard 5

29. (A)—Asking students to reflect on themselves at earlier time would not elicit the most reliable results. (B) and (C) are subjective determinations. (D) is the correct response because any overall student body change in understanding kindness and its importance is likely to show in the data.—Standard 5

30. This question focuses on developing the professional capacity that will promote student success. (A)—Having only one expert on site may prove overwhelming for the individual and slow to get everyone else trained. (B) would produce limited results as some users may be uncomfortable with self-directed learning about technology or using technology. (C) is a missed opportunity to use technology to extend the classroom experience. (D) is a long-term plan that shows the benefits of incorporating new tools in the classroom and providing guidance for beginning users.—Standard 6

31. (A) and (C) would serve to escalate the event. (D) would severely limit the teacher's ability to perform their job. (B) is the correct response because it focuses on

compliance and creating an environment where teachers are held to a high professional standard.—Standard 6

32. (B) and (C) give direction but miss the chance to gain insight on a barrier. (D) lacks holding the teacher to a high professional standard. (A) is the correct response because the teacher can receive support while offering for each student's academic success.—Standard 6

33. While (A), (B), and (C) are all friendly approaches, they do not exhibit the work ethic necessary of a school leader. (D) exhibits strong work ethic and ensures workplace compliance.—Standard 6

34. (B) and (C) will only work to escalate the situation. (D) will include counseling teachers who are not in need. Even in instance where it is not mandated, it is still a courtesy to families to allow consent or withdrawal from the activity of dissecting, so (A) is the correct response.—Standard 6

35. (A) delivers an ambiguous warning. (B) and (D) are ineffective. So (C) is the correct response because it informs the necessary professionals.—Standard 6

36. (B), (C), and (D) only work to escalate the situation, not resolve it. Since the event was not a school function, no laws were broken, no one was harmed, and there was no aggressive action, it is acceptable to take no action, so (A) is the correct response. However, this is a professional you may not want to be associated with.—Standard 7

37. (A), (B), and (C) do not directly stand up for the professional standards set at Principal Jordan's school. (D) is the correct response as it holds everyone involved to a high professional standard.—Standard 7

38. (B), (C), and (D) do not acknowledge the influence leaders have upon their school each day. Every day the leaders in schools everywhere set the stage and the mood for the start of a new school day ripe with possibility. This is also the time of day a teacher or parent can approach a principal with any concerns, and approachability contributes to the success of each student, so (A) is the correct response.—Standard 7

39. (A) and (B) will not improve the situation at all. (C) fails to be accountable and places the responsibility on the parent. (D) is the correct response because it includes reviewing expectations with the teacher and following up to ensure adherence.—Standard 7

40. (A) and (D) delegate the situation to the teacher to handle, but miss the opportunity for professional growth. (B) does not serve to solve the situation. (C) is the correct response because it demonstrates comprehension of how to effectively connect a teach with an appropriate mentor.—Standard 7

41. (A) and (D) merely distract from the issue at hand. (C) does not show unity within the school. (B) is the correct response because it involves setting an example of the desired attribution.—Standard 7

42. (A) does not pertain to the issue, while (C) appreciates the beauty and (D) offers service to the community. (B) provides the most opportunity to learn and give back, so it is the correct response.—Standard 8

43. (B) would be unsafe. (C) and (D) involve taking no action. (A) is the best option for a school plagued by graffiti.—Standard 8

44. (A) and (B) expose the students to the space but misses many opportunities for taking advantage of it. (C) ignores the possibility of the opportunity. (D) is the correct response because it forms a lasting, mutually beneficial relationship between the entities.—Standard 8

45. (B) and (D) would limit the students' exposure to the enjoyment of a full theater production. (C) would prove inconvenient for most involved. (A) is the correct response because it involves exchanging mutually beneficial terms for the school and the community.—Standard 8

46. (A), (B), and (C) are unlikely to enact any positive change on the matter. (D) is the correct response because it connects local students with their community and serves a purpose deemed important by the neighborhood.—Standard 8

47. (A), (B), and (C) do nothing to encourage or support exploring student talents and potential for succeeding in art instruction. (D) is the correct response as it provides the platform for exposing students to art instruction while retaining the flexibility to fit it into the core curriculum.—Standard 10

48. Since it can be a lengthy process to develop a sentiment that permeates throughout a school community, it is unlikely to be quickly undone. But a simple way to spark new interest and connections to the school community is by highlighting achievements or interesting hobbies among the school community, so (A) is the correct response.—Standard 10

49. While (A) and (C) expose the students to new experiences and skills, it is not done so in a formal way and still exposes students only to a limited number of experiences. (D) is the correct response because there is likely to be an eclectic mix of resources and skills offered.—Standard 10

50. While (A) and (C) would certainly help the problem, they may cause great inconvenience or confusion for the parents. (B) is not likely to be enough change to really catch the attention and cause a behavior change in drivers. (D) is the correct choice because it makes student health a priority even at the risk of taking on outraged parents.—Standard 10

51. (A) means to take no action. (B) and (D) do not rely on reasonable measures to achieve the desired outcome. As a matter of student health and sanitary conditions, reporting to the appropriate professionals is warranted and would bring action that enacts change, so (C) is the correct response.—Standard 10

52. (A) and (B) would raise awareness but not funds. (C) would provide student insight on the fundraising process, but would not serve the cause. (D) is the correct response because as students collect coins for the cause, they will be engaging the community and raising awareness on the issue.—Standard 10

53. Acceptable Use policies are written to fully explain the limits and procedures for student use and one important factor that is always included is that students should not expect privacy on these school-owned and -monitored machines, so (B) is unacceptable. The threats made against faculty are both serious and disruptive, so the principal has the right to suspend and/or punish them for this as a separate offense as well as the use of vulgar and sexually offensive language, so (D) and (C) are unacceptable as well. (A) is the best option as it includes the use of a standard operational policy and procedure.—Standard 5

54. Seniority is often used for RIF, but with the more important need to improve student achievement, just submitting a plan based upon it is inadequate; therefore, (A) is not acceptable. (C) does offer an outcome-based look at which teachers have the students with the highest scores, but often this is skewed by some teachers teaching only AP and advanced class while others teaching only introductory classes with high failure rates. (D) is a nonparticipatory approach that reinforces the notion that the principal is not the educational leader there. (B) does involve all stakeholders and offers the best chance for consensus building to improve the school.—Standard 6

55. FERPA and other state laws concerning student information confidentiality outline very clearly when student information is protected and when it is not. (A), (B), and (C) are reasons that will normally allow the contents of student files and conversations to be accessed without parental or student permission. (D) is the best answer as oftentimes employers will request student grades and attendance files for employment decisions. This information cannot be released without a signed release form from the student whose information is being requested.—Standard 2

56. When there is a legal or medical reason for the release of student files, the school will release upon verification of the entity that is requesting it. A search warrant (A), court-ordered subpoena (B), and a parental request (C) are allowable exceptions to the confidentiality rules, but it is never permissible to send additional information to a college or university unless the student has signed a transcript request that will send the final grade report to the school. (D) is the best answer.—Standard 2

57. Every records maintenance policy must include provisions that state how the records will be secured and where (A), who has access and when access is acceptable (B), and how long student confidential information must be kept and when it can be destroyed (D). It is not required that the policy include provisions that records be kept in one particular format. Therefore, (C) is the best answer.—Standard 2

58. (A) When teachers begin to communicate with students for reasons that are not educational, there is the perception that the contact is both inappropriate and unnecessary. That will lead to issues with parents. (D) Social networks often lead to the communication that is viewed by a wider audience than just the teacher and the student and often leads to inappropriate remarks and relationships. (C) Text messages, while convenient, are also stored and recorded in databases of the cellular company and even some innocent communications can be misconstrued as inappropriate—also text messages allow access to information on your phone. (B) is the best answer. Telephone messages on a family phone are acceptable because it is presumed that those messages will be accepted and screened by the parents.—Standard 7

59. (A) It is a good idea to respond to parent face to face or telephone when it is possible, but electronic mail is an effective option. (B) Sending only paper messages is not a viable option as it eliminates the convenience that some parents require when they have to work or need to access note in a more secure setting.

(C) Confidentiality and issues of student privacy will prohibit this option. (D) is the best answer. Signing a communication agreement that each side agrees upon e-mail and contact information will offer opportunities for cooperation between school and home.—Standard 7

60. (A) There is not a requirement for the child to admit that he has been abused to initiate a report to social services, which would lead to an investigation. (B)—It is not the responsibility of the principal to begin the investigation and certainly not contact the spouse to ask her about the incident. (C)—It is inappropriate to transport the child to the police to press charges without notifying the parents, so (D) is the best answer—whenever child abuse or neglect is suspected, it is the law that the school official will report that suspected abuse to child protective services and they will then make a determination whether to investigate or not.—Standard 2

61. (A) Implementing the participation fees will most likely have the effect of reducing participation by low-income students and this would be unacceptable. (B)—Not implementing the policy would also mean ending some of the sports teams and this would have a negative effect on students. (C)—While this seems like a viable option, what would happen if there is only enough money for seven students and ten are in need. (D) is the best answer. The first step is to always seek the input of stakeholders and then develop a plan of action that is fair and equitable.—Standard 3

62. (A)—It is helpful to look at the research, but implementing the strategies without input from other stakeholders risk alienating the others as well as failure. (B)—Looking at other district and school would offer excellent data but selecting a strategy without input is risky. (D) is also ineffective as it limits the range of options based upon the principal's own experiences. (C) is the best answer as it includes all stakeholders in the process of selecting an effective strategy to improve student achievement.—Standard 10

63. (B) is the best answer. Students are permitted to express religious beliefs in their schoolwork, and teachers may not reward or penalize students based solely on their choice to include religious themes or content. A teacher should grade schoolwork with religious content on the same basis as other schoolwork. *Settle v. Dickson County Sch. Bd., 53 F.3d 152 (6th Cir. 1995)* (concluding that a teacher did not violate a ninth-grader's free speech rights by awarding a grade of zero on her research paper on the life of Jesus Christ because the student failed to follow instructions by seeking advance approval of the topic). Because Ms. Smith had not given that stipulation to students, the presentation must be allowed.—Standard 4

64. (D) is the best answer. Merely exposing students to ideas they or their parents find objectionable does not place an unconstitutional burden on students' free exercise of religion when students are not being compelled to affirm or deny a religious belief, nor to perform or not perform a religious exercise. *Leebaert v. Harrington, 332 F.3d 134 (2d Cir. 2003), Mozert v. Hawkins County Bd. Of Educ., 827 F.2d 1058 (6th Cir. 1987)* (upholding required reading assignments, even if textbooks contained material students found objectionable, so long as students were not required to change their beliefs based on the reading).—Standard 3

65. (D) is the best answer. Students may pray in groups during noninstructional time, as long as they are not disruptive and do not harass other students. *Doe v. Duncanville*

Indep. Sch. Dist., 70 F.3d 402 (5th Cir. 1995). For example, group prayer during lunch time, in common areas, or at the flag pole are all permissible practices. A public school student has an absolute right to individually, voluntarily, and silently pray or meditate in school in a manner that does not disrupt the instructional or other activities of the school. A person may not require, encourage, or coerce a student to engage in or refrain from such prayer or meditation during any school activity. Nothing in the U.S. Constitution prohibits any public school student from voluntarily praying at any time before, during, or after the school day. *Santa Fe Indep. Sch. Dist. v. Doe, 530 U.S. 290 (2000)*. (A) would limit that freedom and is not acceptable. (B)—The sheer chaos that would result from numerous schedule changes would impact instruction—so that is not an acceptable option. (C)—This may be viewed as segregating the group, so it is not acceptable.—Standard 3

66. (D) is the best answer. Graduation speeches cannot contain sectarian or proselytizing language if the speeches are properly characterized as school sponsored. For example, a California appellate court permitted a school district to edit the content of commencement addresses because the content of the speech was sectarian. The court held that the degree of school sponsorship and control over the speech made it state-sponsored speech. Consequently, to permit students to deliver sectarian speeches would have violated the Establishment Clause. *Cole v. Oroville Union High Sch. Dist., 228 F.3d 1092 (9th Cir. 2000)*. See also *Lassonde v. Pleasanton Unified Sch. Dist., 320 F.3d 979 (9th Cir. 2003)* (upholding a school district's decision to edit proselytizing text from a student's graduation speech). (A) is not an option as a graduation speech is school sponsored.—Standard 4

67. This question focuses on establishing a coherent system of curriculum that benefits each child. (B), (C), and (D) miss taking advantage of an opportunity for academic growth within the school. (A) allows teachers to collaborate and then work together to develop cohesive units of instruction.—Standard 4

68. (D) is the best answer. Student clubs of a religious nature must be permitted to meet on school property, subject to the same rules and privileges as other non-curricular student groups. In secondary schools, student-organized, student-led groups meet pursuant to school district policies established under the federal Equal Access Act. 20 U.S.C. § 4071. Under the Equal Access Act, employees may be present at student religious meetings only in a nonparticipatory capacity. 20 U.S.C. § 4071(c) (3). In both elementary and secondary schools, community groups, including adult-led groups attended by students, such as the Good News Club or the Boy Scouts, meet on campus pursuant to school district policy. Under the First Amendment, these policies must be viewpoint neutral; schools must permit community groups that espouse religious viewpoints to have the same access to school facilities as that extended to community groups espousing secular viewpoints. *Good News Club v. Milford Cent. Sch., 533 U.S. 98 (2001)*; *Lamb's Chapel v. Center Moriches Union Free Sch. Dist., 508 U.S. 384 (1993)*.—Standard 3

69. (D) is the best answer. Most educational research on religion and how it can be taught in schools insures that schools study religion and do not sponsor the practice of religion.—Standard 4

70. (B) is the best answer. Title VI of the Civil Rights Act of 1964, 42 U.S.C. § 2000d, 34 C.F.R. Part 100, prohibiting discrimination based on national origin, is

interpreted by the Office for Civil Rights of the U.S. Department of Education as requiring that schools provide non-English-speaking parents with adequate notice concerning school programs and activities, presumably including disciplinary procedures. See also 20 U.S.C. § 1703(f) (obligation of schools to remove language barriers). Thus, a school's failure to make its rules available in a language that the student understands could provide a basis for challenging disciplinary action. The same is true of a school's failure to translate important disciplinary notices, or to provide interpreter services, if needed, at disciplinary hearings.—Standard 5

71. (A) is the best answer. In *Vernonia School District v. Acton (1995)*, the Supreme Court has ruled in favor of the school district on random drug testing of student-athletes. Schools must balance students' right to privacy against the need to make school campuses safe and keep student-athletes away from drugs, the court said. The drug-testing policy, which required students to provide a urine sample, involved only a limited invasion of privacy, according to the justices: "Students who voluntarily participate in school athletics have reason to expect intrusions upon normal rights and privileges, including privacy." The court noted that student-athletes have even fewer privacy rights, the justices said, and must follow rules that don't apply to other students. Joining a team usually requires getting a physical exam, obtaining insurance coverage, and maintaining a minimum grade point average. More recently, the court has ruled in favor of school policies requiring random drug testing for all extracurricular activities (*Board of Education v. Earls, 2002*).—Standard 3

72. (D) is the best answer. Courts have determined that schools could punish students for the content of their underground newspapers. The case of Justin Boucher is a prime example. When he was a junior at a Wisconsin public high school, Boucher wrote and distributed a publication named *The Last*. It featured numerous anonymous articles on a variety of subjects. The publication's stated purpose was to "ruffle a few feathers and jump-start some to action." Under the pseudonym of Sacco and Vanzetti (two Italian anarchists sentenced to death in the 1920s—many believe unfairly), Boucher wrote an article, "So You Want to Be a Hacker," which told students "how to hack the school's gay ass computers." School officials expelled Boucher for endangering school property. Boucher countered that his article was mere advocacy protected by the First Amendment. A district judge granted Boucher an injunction, but the school successfully appealed to the 7th Circuit in *Boucher v. School Board of the School District of Greenfield*. The appeals court wrote in its 1998 opinion that the hacker article "purports to be a blueprint for the invasion of Greenfield's [the high school's] computer system along with encouragement to do just that." As such, the court ruled that it was reasonable for school officials to believe the article would cause a substantial disruption of school activities.—Standard 2

73. (D) is the best answer. Some courts have sided with the students, saying that school officials may not censor student speech unless they can reasonably forecast that the speech will cause a substantial disruption of the school environment or invade the rights of others. Other courts and commentators have said that school officials simply lack the authority to regulate students' off-campus behavior—on or off the Internet. In 2002 the Pennsylvania Supreme Court reached the

opposite conclusion in another student Internet speech case. The case involved a web site created by Justin Swidler that contained derogatory comments about a math teacher and the principal. Much of the site was devoted to ridiculing the math teacher, comparing her to Adolf Hitler, and making fun of her appearance. The site even contained a phrase that said, "Give me $20 to help pay for the hitman." School officials expelled Swidler, citing the extreme emotional distress suffered by the math teacher and the disruption the web site caused at the school. Swidler argued in a lawsuit that his web page was a form of protected speech. The Pennsylvania courts, including the Pennsylvania Supreme Court in 2002, sided with the school district in *J.S. v. Bethlehem Area School District*. In examining the case, the state high court first determined whether the speech was a true threat. School officials argued the speech was a true threat, focusing on the language about paying $20 for a hitman. However, the high court disagreed, writing: "We believe that the Web site, taken as a whole, was a sophomoric, crude, highly offensive and perhaps misguided attempt to humor or parody. However, it did not reflect a serious expression of intent to inflict harm." The high court then determined whether school officials had the authority to regulate the student's web site. Swidler argued that the web site was beyond school officials' control because he created it off-campus. The court disagreed, writing: "We find there is a sufficient nexus between the web site and the school campus to consider the speech as occurring on-campus." The court determined the speech occurred on campus because the student accessed the site at school, showed it to a fellow student and informed other students of the site. "We hold that where speech that is aimed at a specific school and/or its personnel is brought onto the school campus or accessed at school by its originator, the speech will be considered on-campus speech," the court wrote.—Standard 2

74. (A), (B), and (C) are essential parts of an effective anti-bullying program that will allow students to develop skills to prevent and deal with this actions. While it is the older acceptable method of meeting violence with violence, (D) is not acceptable and therefore is the best answer.—Standard 5

75. (A) is the best answer. School officials cannot pull books off library shelves simply because they dislike the ideas in those books. In *Board of Education v. Pico*, the Supreme Court ruled that school officials in New York violated the First Amendment by removing several books from junior high school library shelves for being too controversial. The court said the First Amendment protects students' right to receive information and ideas and that the principal place for such information is the library. However, in *Pico*, the Supreme Court also said school officials could remove books from library shelves if they were "pervasively vulgar." The court noted that its decision did not involve school officials' control over the curriculum or even the acquisition of books for school libraries.—Standard 4

76. (D) is the best answer. The raging debate over gay and lesbian student clubs often features Equal Access Act disputes. In some communities, students have formed gay and lesbian or gay-straight alliance clubs to promote greater tolerance toward gays and lesbians. These clubs have often met harsh resistance from other students, parents, community leaders, and school officials. In another 2003 case, *Boyd County High School Gay-Straight Alliance v. Board of Education of*

Boyd County, a federal judge in Kentucky ruled that school officials violated the Equal Access Act when they refused to give a gay-straight alliance club the same opportunities as other noncurriculum-related student clubs. The stated purpose of the club was "to provide students with a safe haven to talk about anti-gay harassment and to work together to promote tolerance, understanding and acceptance of one another regardless of sexual orientation." The school argued that it was justified in preventing the club from meeting because of the disruptions caused by other students who vigorously opposed the club. These students protested by wearing shirts saying "Adam and Eve, not Adam and Steve." On one school day, half of the students did not attend, many in protest of the gay-straight club. These disruptions caused school officials to suspend all noncurriculum-related schools. However, the gay-straight alliance alleged that school officials, despite the school board's supposed suspension of clubs, still allowed many student groups to meet at Boyd County High School. These clubs included the Drama Club, the Bible Club, the Executive Councils, and the Beta Club. U.S. District Judge David L. Bunning sided with the student club, finding that school officials violated the Equal Access Act by treating the gay-straight alliance group differently from other student clubs. The judge rejected the school board's argument that it could prohibit the gay-straight club because it caused substantial disruption of school activities under the Equal Access Act.—Standard 3

77. (D) is the best answer. Most public school programs operate for approximately 180 days per year. Parents and educators have argued that, for some children with disabilities, particularly those with severe and multiple disabilities, a 180-day school year is not sufficient to meet their needs. In *Armstrong v. Kline* (1979), the parents of five students with severe disabilities claimed that their children tended to regress during the usual breaks in the school year and called on the schools to provide a period of instruction longer than 180 days. The court agreed and ordered the schools to extend the school year for these students. Several states and local districts now provide year-round educational programs for some students with disabilities, but there are no clear and universally accepted guidelines as to which students are entitled to free public education for a longer-than-usual school year. (A)—School districts must find the funds if the IEP list extended school years as a requirement for the students. (B)—Free and appropriate means without cost—they cannot be charged for services to serve their students. (C)—It is illegal to suggest that a parent withdraw their special education student to gain services.—Standard 4

78. (C) is the best answer. The principal has the legal authority to insure that the school has a safe and orderly environment that is conducive to learning. If the principal believes their presence there will jeopardize other students or faculty, he can remove them from school. (A)—Not valid as the principal does have the authority, but it cannot be based upon the fact that they had been in trouble previously. (B)—Not valid as the principal does have the authority. (D)—Sending the students to alternative school is a change in placement and requires approval from the school board.—Standard 4

79. (D) is the best answer. While the U.S. Constitution upholds the right to be safe from unreasonable searches and seizures, the standard for school searches

is less rigid. The search is lawful if the school has a "reasonable suspicion" that a school rule has been violated. This means the search must be justified when made and reasonably related to the circumstances being investigated. For example, a student is believed to have been smoking on campus, but denies it. A reasonable search can be made of the purse or backpack he or she was carrying at the time of the incident. His or her locker and pockets can also be legally searched. Courts will weigh a student's right to privacy against a school's need to obtain evidence of school rule violations and violations of the law. This "reasonable suspicion" standard has been upheld in challenges to locker, desk, and car searches. (A)—This is not an option as it would seem to be preferential. (B)—This would also be seen as preferential and is unacceptable. (C)—Parents do not have the authority to demand students open their personal belonging.—Standard 2

80. This question underscores the need for public relations and professional support. Responses (A) and (B) suggest a defensive response. Response (C) violates the collaborative spirit of school improvement. Response (D) is correct because it satisfies the school's apparent need for shared staff involvement and professional support.—Standards 4 and 10

81. One of the keys to the success of curriculum implementation is training and involving staff in the process. Response (A) is too superficial. Responses (C) and (D) do not encourage ownership and invite staff input. The correct response is (B), allowing sufficient time for the training of staff and the integration of curriculum.—Standards 4 and 6

82. (A) is the best answer. Under FERPA, parents or eligible students have the right to inspect and review the student's education records maintained by the school. Schools are not required to provide copies of records unless, for reasons such as great distance, it is impossible for parents or eligible students to review the records. Schools may charge a fee for copies.—Standard 8

83. The best answer is (A)—The most important feature is to include multiple strategies to communicate with parents and insure that they become aware of the strategies. Often the most difficult obstacle is insuring that the information gets to the parents in a format that they understand and can relate to their children. A systematic approach will allow for this to happen.—Standard 3

84. The best answer is (B)—Walk-throughs are not part of a formal evaluation process and should be an opportunity for teachers and students to maintain contact with the principal and other administrators. It is important that each walk-through has a focus and teachers understand that they will be used as an opportunity for reflective growth rather than formal evaluation.—Standard 4

85. The best answer is (B)—as the host the principal is within his responsibilities to insure the meeting is adequately supplied and goes smoothly. His suggestion asks for a higher level of respect rather than demands it. (A)—Unacceptable as it does not afford the level of support that any other keynote speaker would receive. (C)—Taking over the meeting and the microphone would lead to a further deterioration of her status and ability to lead. (D)—Ending the meeting also would send the message that they do not want a female supervisor.—Standard 8

Scoring CR Question Two: Answers should include the following in their discussion:

1. Specifically addresses Professional Development/Training Issues
2. Recognizes difficulty of change or fear of risks (ingrained practices)
3. Teachers playing it safe for evaluation observations
4. Belief that cooperative learning doesn't work for certain students
5. Difficulty implementing cooperative learning because of classroom management issues

Standard 2.b,d

Std. 2.b Align and focus systems of curriculum, instruction, and assessment within and across grade levels to promote student academic success, love of learning, the identities and habits of learners, and healthy sense of self.

Std. 2.d Ensure instructional practice that is intellectually challenging and authentic to student experiences, recognizes student strengths, and is differentiated and personalized.

Practice Constructed-response Essay Questions

Answers after each Question

The standards associated with each question are not limited to the ones listed. You are encouraged to develop connections with additional standards. Developing these connections the way you perceive education and the way you frame issues of educational practice will be through the reading and understanding of the ISLLC Standards.

Write your response to the following constructed-response questions. On the actual test, there are seven constructed-response questions. Below are 15 essay questions to practice. Suggested time for each question is 10–12 minutes.

Question 1: Herbert Hoover High School is a very diverse school. It is cultural and socially diverse with pupils from a variety of backgrounds. There is a significant amount of students who are African-Americans; they make up 20 percent of the school student body. A group of African-American parents have approached you about the current curriculum. They are unhappy about the contents of the curriculum and claim that it does not reflect African-American history and culture. They explain that the curriculum is no longer relevant to the students in the school. They are worried that their children may lose a sense of their identity and not be aware of their heritage. They explain that the curriculum that is laid down by the school district has not been updated since 2005. The African-American parents are not content with this, and they want more information and instruction for their children on African-American culture. They claim that because the curriculum does not adequately represent the African-American experience, the school is failing to fulfill its own policy of inclusivity. The principal explains that the school has a policy of cultural sensitivity and would address this issue by the next parent-teacher association meeting.

What are the first steps to be taken? How should the principal address parents' demands? What steps can the principal take to assure the parents that the school is inclusive?
Explain curricular or learning programs that the principal can propose so that Herbert Hoover High School can improve?

Scoring CR Question One: Answers discuss the following, but are not limited to:

1. Well-developed analysis and synthesis of all perspectives about the curriculum
2. Understanding that the district curriculum is outdated and needs to be inclusive
3. Describing challenges faced by the school
4. Evaluating an improvement plan (strengths and weaknesses)
5. Multiple ways to elicit community support
6. Multiple actions principals should take to improve the curriculum
7. _____

Question 2: A new principal is hired at Diego Rivera Elementary School. The parent-teacher organization (PTO) is run by a few wealthy families who dictate what programs are offered for the students and what languages the school offers. They have gotten Chinese as the only foreign language being offered in the elementary school, because the higher incomes parents go on many business trips to China. However, the lower income students who make up 64 percent of the student body come from the Caribbean and their parents speak Spanish, but are often at work during PTO meetings and cannot contribute to these decisions. Additionally, the owners of local stores and 52 percent of the teachers at the school speak Spanish as either their primary or secondary language.

What leadership position should the principal take to resolve this disparity and what language should the school offer in order to benefit the students and community most?

Scoring CR Question Two: Answers should include the following in their discussion:

Response specifically cites the civil and/or equity rights of parents and students, and includes at least one of the following:

• Meeting with both of the parent and student groups to discuss the objections
• Suggesting some alternatives for the school
• Examining the content of the foreign language class to determine the reasoning behind offering it and its appropriateness for all students

---

Question 3: The municipal health department is encouraging schools to offer healthier options for school lunches, particularly in low-income areas, where parents cannot afford healthier foods and child obesity is high. The president of the school board has had the school contracted to Snaxdepot to provide school lunches for the past 20 years. The public health department is trying to tackle childhood obesity and it's at 34 percent at Elizabeth Cady Stanton Elementary School. Child obesity has hit an all-time high, and it has impacted this elementary school the most. Snaxdepot insists on adding high-fructose corn syrup to many of its food options, even sandwiches, to ensure that these foods are appealing to children. Eighty-six percent of children at Elizabeth Cady Stanton Elementary School participate in the state government–funded Free-and-Reduced Lunch program. The faculty and staff, who know that students will have higher educational outcomes and be able to focus for longer periods of time, believe that they should look for another school lunch provider aligned with public health department's provisions for healthier lunches. The president of the school board refuses their first appeal, arguing that the school cannot afford a contract with any other provider for the quality of food that they are requesting.

How should the administration handle the need for children to have healthier options and the school board insisting they stick with a corporate contract? Propose three possible actions in which the administration can provide the most benefit for their students?

Scoring CR Question Three: Answers should include the following in their discussion:

Response specifically cites the need to avoid the appearance of impropriety, that is, unethical behavior or actions suggesting a conflict of interest in awarding contracts, plus at least one concern related to the process or consequences of making such a purchase such as:

- The importance of both price and service elements
- The possibility that specific guidelines exist for a purchase over a certain amount
- Potential problems involving the school board member that could occur

---

Question 4: The school system in San Joaquin is facing major budget cuts. The school board decides to cut all arts and extracurricular programming from the schools. The students and parents are concerned that this will affect students' ability to be involved and their college applications. This also has the potential to impact the percentage of college acceptances that schools receive, which could further divert funding away from the school. The administrations of all the schools have formed a committee to find a solution that will appeal to the parents but also work within the constraints of the school board.

What should the committee prioritize?
What possible solutions should the committee propose? Create a possible timeline of probable actions to take.

Scoring CR Question Four: Answers should include the following in their discussion:

Response both discusses specific instructional issues related to arts curricula and increasing college enrollment and presents advice on how the administration can deal with these instruction-based issues in the school and within the school district. The instructional issues should be related to topics relevant to art, extracurricular activities, and increased college enrollment and may include, but are not limited to, such areas as human development, healthy mental development, and high-stakes testing. Issues of educational equity, Standard 3, should be included in the answer as this school could be in a low-socioeconomic-status community.

Response recognizes that this situation presents itself as a genuine learning opportunity or a "teachable moment" in recognizing school budget cuts and needs of the community, increased community involvement on many levels of participation, and possibly getting the school board involved.

Question 5: A long-time vice principal is stuck with a dilemma the week before classes start. It has been a very rainy week at John F. Kennedy High School and the faculty have received funding for a grant that will allow them to fund laptops for incoming freshmen. However, the maintenance department head with the school business administrator have used some of the funds allocated for student laptops to fix a leak in the ceiling. The two vice principals are tasked with resolving the issue. The newly hired vice principal says that since the school is opening in a week, the ceiling needs to be fixed and that he is sure the school can find funds to allocate laptops to student once they apply for maintenance funding from the municipality.

How will the long-time vice principal navigate through this issue? Propose two possible solutions.

Q5: Std. 9.k Develop and administer systems for fair and equitable management of conflict among students, faculty and staff, leaders, families, and community

Std. 9.d Are responsible, ethical, and accountable stewards of the school's monetary and nonmonetary resources engaging in effective budgeting and accounting practices.

Question 6: A tenured mathematics teacher, Mr. Fitzgerald, at Jacqueline Onassis High School calls the assistant principal in charge of his department, Mrs. Kennedy, on a Monday morning notifying her that he will be late. Mrs. Kennedy arrives at Mr. Fitzgerald's first period class, who is supposed to have a quiz. After half an hour Mr. Fitzgerald arrives and greets Mrs. Kennedy in the front of the classroom. Mrs. Kennedy can smell alcohol from his breath and he is visibly inebriated. She tells him he needs to make copies of the quiz and then go to the staff lounge. The quiz is administered, but Mr. Fitzgerald asks Mrs. Kennedy not to tell the administration.

What should Mrs. Kennedy do?

What administrative consequences should Mr. Fitzgerald face? Create a dialogue between Mr. Fitzgerald and the administration to resolve this issue.

Q6: Std. 9.k

Std. 9.k Develop and administer systems for fair and equitable management of conflict among students, faculty and staff, leaders, families, and community.

Question 7: The students at Oprah Gail Winfrey Middle School are in the middle of completing the annual standardized assessment test, when the fire alarm goes off. Thankfully, it was a false alarm. Most of the teachers decided to respect the rule of the school and evacuated their students. However, five teachers, in different parts of the school, decided to tell their students to ignore the alarm because they felt that it was a false alarm and they did not want their students to forfeit their testing for the day. The principal finds out about what happens.

What actions should the principal take with regard to the five teachers who did not follow school safety procedures? Then, how should the principal handle the interruption in the annual state-mandated testing?

Q7: Std. 4.a, g

Std. 4.a Implement coherent systems of curriculum, instruction, and assessment that promote the mission, vision, and core values of the school, embody high expectations for student learning, align with academic standards, and are culturally responsive.

Std. 4.g Use assessment data appropriately and within technical limitations to monitor student progress and improve instruction.

Question 8: It has come to the attention of the principal that a student, with the full support of her parents, has surreptitiously video-taped a teacher engaged in teaching a lesson in order to gather evidence of the teacher's perceived incompetence. The school district has a policy in place forbidding the video-recording of lessons in this manner.

What should be the first steps taken to resolve this situation?
Discuss how the principal should respond to this situation.

Q8: Std. 8.b, c

Std. 8.b Create and sustain positive, collaborative, and productive relationships with families and the community for the benefit of students.

Std. 8.c Engage in regular and open two-way communication with families and the community about the school, students, needs, problems, and accomplishments.

Question 9: Hart High School has always had an open-door policy and encouraged parent participation in the building. This policy has recently been tested, however, by several parents who have demonstrated behavior in the building associated with overbearing or "helicopter" parents. The situation came to a head when a verbal and physical altercation arose during a student Step Dancing Club practice.

What is the best approach to deal with this issue?

Discuss how the principal should resolve this challenge.

Q9: Std. 8.b, c

Std. 8.b Create and sustain positive, collaborative, and productive relationships with families and the community for the benefit of students.

Std. 8.c Engage in regular and open two-way communication with families and the community about the school, students, needs, problems, and accomplishments.

Question 10: Auditorium space is limited at John Brown High School. There are times when the band is scheduled to rehearse for a concert, only to find the auditorium stage filled with drama props. Band rehearsal has been moved to the gym, but this results in gym classes being displaced. Explain how a principal can resolve this issue.

Q.10: Std. 9.c

Std. 9.c Establish and sustain a professional culture of engagement and commitment to shared vision, goals, and objectives pertaining to the education of the whole child; high expectations for professional work; ethical and equitable practice; trust and open communication; and collaboration, collective efficacy, and continuous individual and organizational learning and improvement.

Question 11: Tewanna Douglass has always considered herself a progressive and able school principal. However, with the ever-growing emphasis on academic improvement, community involvement, professional training, and accountability, she has found herself increasingly isolated from the administrative duties that she has traditionally performed. For example, she spends many hours isolated in her office doing paperwork and now delegates additional responsibilities to her administrative staff. Discuss ways in which the principal can address this problem.

Q11: Std. 9.a

Std. 9.a Institute, manage, and monitor operations and administrative systems that promote the mission and vision of the school.

Question 12: Recent educational reform and budget restrictions have resulted in the elimination of school programs and elective classes. Lately, the high school principal has received complaints made by the teachers that students are being placed in visual or performing arts classes, such as art and music. These students who have no discern-ableability and display a lack of desire in the arts are being placed in these classes. List the steps that you would take and explain how the principal should address this issue.

Q12: Std. 4.a, d

Std. 4.a Implement coherent systems of curriculum, instruction, and assessment that promote the mission, vision, and core values of the school, embody high expectations for student learning, align with academic standards, and are culturally responsive.

Std. 4.d Ensure instructional practice that is intellectually challenging, authentic to student experiences, recognizes student strengths, and is differentiated and personalized.

Question 13: Ms. Lindsey, the young high school English teacher, makes it a point not to "friend" students or their parents on Facebook©. Once the school year is over, the students are no longer her students nor are their parents, so she "friends" them on Facebook©. In September, Ms. Lindsey went out drinking with friends and she posts pictures of herself and others at a club on the outskirts of town. The pictures posted are not vulgar nor sexually explicit in content. However, the comments made under-neath the pictures suggest that Ms. Lindsey had not conducted herself in a respectful manner.

A parent, Pamela Smith, had an older son who graduated from high school and had friended Ms. Lindsey, last year. Ms. Smith "friended" the English teacher on Face-book last June. This year, Pamela's younger son is in Ms. Lindsey's English class. Mrs. Smith brought the Facebook© incident to the attention of the school principal, Mrs. Hughes. Pamela Smith wants her son removed from Ms. Lindsey's English class immediately. The mother claims she wants her son removed due to the fact that this conduct is unbecoming of a school teacher. Mrs. Smith also claimed that Ms. Lindsey is not fit to be a teacher as her behavior outside of school is inappropriate for a school staff member.

How should the school principal approach this issue?
With whom should the school principal have a dialogue?
What could be done to prevent a future incident such as this one from arising?

Q13: Std. 2.a, f

Std. 2.a Act ethically and professionally in personal conduct, relationships with oth-ers, decision making, stewardship of the school's resources, and all aspects of school leadership.

Std. 2.f Provide moral direction for the school and promote ethical and professional behavior among faculty and staff.

Question 14: The Roosevelt High School has always had a good reputation in its area. One of the school's younger teachers is very popular with the students and he is a very effective educator. He has been a staff member for two years, but has already become a valued member of the teaching staff. It has been brought to the attention of the school principal by some parents at a recent parent-teacher meeting that this teacher has been in contact with his pupils on various social media platforms such as Facebook, after school. They have been informed by their children that they often communicate with their teacher about things other than their school work on social media. The parents are worried that this may be improper and they are concerned that it is not appropriate for a teacher to be so friendly with their children, who are impressionable teenagers.

The school, like other public schools, has a code of ethics for teachers, including how they should interact with pupils after school hours. The young teacher has not apparently done anything wrong, but the parents are concerned and they are requesting for consultation on the use of social media by teachers in general, especially with regard to communication with students.

What issues should the principal discuss with the young teacher about his use of social media?

How would you dispel the fears of the parents with regard to social media communications among teachers and pupils?

Q14: Std. 2.f

Std. 2.f Provide moral direction for the school and promote ethical and professional behavior among faculty and staff.

Question 15: It has been brought to the attention of the Clara Barton Middle School that cyberbullying is a problem. Many students are being bullied online or are bullying others online. Technology has given bullies a platform to torment their victims via social media, texting, and other digital means. One case, in particular, has alarmed many in the school. Hallie, a teenage transgender girl, has been the victim of a hate campaign. Her school work has suffered and she no longer wants to attend school. The school has taken the responsibility to prevent cyberbullying for this student and others. The parents are concerned about Hallie's academic achievement and mental well-being.

The fact that some laws are pending enactment in relation to cyberbullying is challenging since parents, teachers, and administrators are unsure of how to legally handle such issues. The school district has addressed this issue by teaching students how to use the Internet in a sensitive and responsible way. However, the problems of cyberbullying have only increased and this would indicate that the school's previous efforts have not met the challenge. There clearly needs to be something done to end the cyberbullying for the gender-nonconforming teenagers, as Hallie is not the only one who has experienced cyberbullying due to her identity. There are many instances when similar bullying has led to suicide of victims. Due to the potential consequences, it is imperative that the school take immediate action in order to prevent this from happening.

Create a timeline with three main priorities for the school principal to implement within the school year.

How can the school make a difference regarding this issue?

What interventions can the school principal take to limit or end the rampant cyberbullying?

What stakeholders should be involved in the initiative to resolve homophobic cyber-bullying? And what actions should they take?

Standards 2.d; 3.d, e

Std. 2.d Safeguard and promote the values of democracy, individual freedom and responsibility, equity, social justice, community, and diversity.

Std. 3.d Develop student policies and address student misconduct in a positive, fair, and unbiased manner.

Std. 3.e Confront and alter institutional biases of student marginalization, deficit-based schooling, and low expectations associated with race, class, culture and language, gender and sexual orientation, and disability or special status.

Notes

SECTION 2

1. "School Leadership Series," *Educational Testing Service*, https://www.ets.org/sls/states/
2. "Understanding Your School Leadership Series Scores 2015–16," *ETS*, http://www.ets.org/s/sls/pdf/uysls_1516.pdf
3. "Fees," *ETS*, https://www.ets.org/sls/about/fees/
4. "School Leaders Licensure Assessment," *ETS School Leadership Series*, https://www.ets.org/s/sls/pdf/6011.pdf
5. "Accommodations for Test Takers with Disabilities or Health-related Needs," *ETS School Leadership Series*, http://www.ets.org/praxis/register/disabilities/
6. "Bulletin Supplement for Test Takers with Disabilities or Health-Related Needs," *ETS*, http://www.ets.org/s/disabilities/pdf/bulletin_supplement_test_takers_with_disabilities_health_needs.pdf
7. "Understanding Your School Leadership Series Scores 2015–16," *ETS*, http://www.ets.org/s/sls/pdf/uysls_1516.pdf
8. "Frequently Asked Questions," *ETS*, http://www.ets.org/sls/faq

SECTION 4

1. National Policy Board for Educational Administration (2015). *Professional Standards for Educational Leaders*. Reston, VA: Author.

SECTION 5

1. "Steps to Test Taking Success." *US News*, http://www.usnews.com/education/best-graduate-schools/test prep/articles/2010/05/28/test-prep-7-tips-for-success?page=3

SECTION 6

1. Martin, Emmie, "4 ways to outsmart any multiple-choice test," *Business Insider*, http://www.businessinsider.com/4-ways-to-outsmart-any-multiple-choice-test-2015-6.

SECTION 8

1. "American Test Anxieties Association," AMTAA, http://www.amtaa.org/index.html
2. "Performance Expectations and Indicators for Education Leaders," Council of Chief State School Officers (CCSSO), National Policy Board for Education Administration, http://www.ccsso.org/Documents/2015/Peformance_Indicators_2015.pdf
3. "ISLLC Standards," Florida Gulf Coast University, http://coe.fgcu.edu/faculty/valesky/isllcstandards.html
4. "Professional Standards for Educational Leaders 2015," Council of Chief State School Officers (CCSSO), National Policy Board for Education Administration, . pdf file.

SECTION 9

1. Patel, Neil. "When, How, and How Often to Take a Break," Inc., http://www.inc.com/neil-patel/when-how-and-how-often-to-take-a-break.html
2. "Computer Vision Syndrome," American Optometric Association, http://www.aoa.org/patients-and-public/caring-for-your-vision/protecting-your-vision/computer-vision-syndrome?sso=y
3. "How Fast Can You Read This?" *Wall Street Journal*, http://projects.wsj.com/speedread/
4. "Dealing with Study Burnout," Albert Einstein College of Medicine, https://www.einstein.yu.edu/education/student-affairs/academic-support-counseling/medical-school-challenges/study-burnout.aspx
5. "12 Tips for Surviving and Thriving in Grad School," Psych Central, http://psychcentral.com/lib/12-tips-for-surviving-and-thriving-in-grad-school/

SECTION 10

1. "School Leaders Licensure Assessment," ETS School Leadership Series, https://www.ets.org/s/sls/pdf/6011.pdf
2. "Find a Study Buddy," MoocLab, http://www.mooclab.club/pages/study_buddy/
3. Twitter, https://twitter.com/search?q=SLLA%20test&src=typd
4. MeetUp, http://www.meetup.com/
5. "Test-taking Strategies," Brigham Young University, https://casc.byu.edu/testtaking-strategies

Bibliography

Adams, C. M., Forsyth, P. B., & Mitchell, R. M. (2009). The formation of parent-school trust: A multilevel analysis. *Educational Administration Quarterly, 45*(1), 4–33.

Beck, L. G. (1994). *Reclaiming educational administration as a caring profession.* New York, NY: Teachers College Press.

Bogotch, I. E. (2002). Educational leadership and social justice: Practice into theory. *Journal of School Leadership, 12*(2), 138–156.

Brooks, J. S., Jean-Marie, G., Normore, A., & Hodgins, D. (2007). Distributed leadership for social justice: Exploring how influence and equity are stretched over an urban high school. *Journal of School Leadership, 17*(4), 378–408.

Brooks, J. S., Scribner, J. P., & Eferakorho, J. (2004). Teacher leadership in the context of whole school reform. *Journal of School Leadership, 14*(3), 242–265.

Brown, K. M., Benkovitz, J., Muttillo, A. J., & Urban, T. (2011). Leading schools of excellence and equity: Documenting effective strategies in closing achievement gaps. *Teachers College Record, 113*(1), 57–96.

Bryk, A. S., & Schneider, B. (2002). *Trust in schools: A core resource for improvement.* New York, NY: Russell Sage.

Bryk, A. S., Sebring, P. B., Allensworth, E., Luppescu, S., & Easton, J. (2010). *Organizing schools for improvement: Lessons from Chicago.* Chicago, IL: University of Chicago Press.

Cairney, T. H. (2000). Beyond the classroom walls: The rediscovery of the family and community as partners in education. *Educational Review, 52*(2), 163–174.

Cooper, C. W. (2009). Performing culture work in demographically changing schools: Implications for expanding transformative leadership frameworks. *Educational Administration Quarterly, 45*(5), 694–724.

Cosner, S. (2011). Supporting the initiation and early development of evidence-based grade-level collaboration in urban elementary schools: Key roles and strategies of principals and literacy coordinators. *Urban Education, 46*(4), 786–827.

Drago-Severson, E. (2004). *Helping teachers learn: Principal leadership for adult growth and development.* Thousand Oaks, CA: Corwin.

Drago-Severson, E. (2012). New opportunities for principal leadership: Shaping school climates for enhanced teacher development. *Teachers College Record, 114*(3), 1–44.

Enomoto, E. (1997). Negotiating the ethics of care and justice. *Educational Administration Quarterly, 33*(3), 351–370.

Enomoto, E., Karner, B., & Starratt, R. J. (2007). *Leading through the quagmire: Ethical foundations, critical methods, and practical applications for school leadership.* Lanham, MD: Rowman & Littlefield.

Evans, A. E. (2007). School leaders and their sensemaking about race and demographic change. *Educational Administration Quarterly,* 43(2), 159–188.

ETS. (2015). *Frequently asked questions.* Retrieved from http://www.ets.org/sls/faq

ETS. (2015). Understanding Your School Leadership Series Scores 2015–16. Retrieved from http://www.ets.org/s/sls/pdf/uysls_1516.pdf

Fan, X., & Chen, M. (2001). Parental involvement and students' academic achievement: A metaanalysis. *Educational Psychology Review,* 13(1), 1–22.

Feuerstein, A. (2000). School characteristics and parent involvement: Influences on participation in children's schools. *Journal of Educational Research,* 94(1), 29–40.

Four Tests. (2015). SLLA Exam. Retrieved from https://www.4tests.com/slla.

Garet, M. S., Porter, A. C., Desimore, L., Birman, B. F., & Yoon, K. S. (2001). What makes professional development effective? Results from a national sample of teachers.*American Educational Research Journal,* 38(4), 915–945.

Goddard, R. D., Salloum, S. J., & Berebitsky, D. (2009). Trust as a mediator of the relationships between poverty, racial, composition, and academic achievement. *Educational Administration Quarterly,* 45(2), 292–311.

Goddard, Y. L., Neumerski, C. M., Goddard, R. D., Salloum, S. J., & Berebitsky, D. (2010). A multilevel exploratory study of the relationship between teachers' perceptions of principals' instructional support and group norms for instruction in elementary schools. *Elementary School Journal,* 111(2), 336–357.

Goddard, R., Goddard, Y., Kim, E. S., & Miller, R. (2015). A theoretical and empirical analysis of the roles of instructional leadership, teacher collaboration, and collective efficacy beliefs in support of student learning. *American Journal of Education,* 121(4), 501–530.

Gordon, M. F., & Louis, K. S. (2009). Linking parent and community involvement with student achievement: Comparing principal and teacher perceptions of stakeholder influence. *American Journal of Education,* 116(1), 1–31.

Grissom, J. A. (2011). Can good principals keep teachers in disadvantaged schools? Linking principal effectiveness to teacher satisfaction and turnover in hard-to-staff environments. *Teachers College Record,* 113(11), 2552–2585.

Grissom, J. A., & Loeb, S. (2011). Triangulating principal effectiveness: How perspectives of parents, teachers, and assistant principals identify the central importance of managerial skills. *American Educational Research Journal,* 48(5), 1091–1123.

Halverson, R. (2010). School formative feedback systems. *Peabody Journal of Education,* 85(2), 130–146.

Halverson, R., Grigg, J., Prichett, R., & Thomas, C. (2007). The new instructional leadership: Creating data-driven instructional systems in school. *Journal of School Leadership,* 17(2), 159–194.

Howard, T. C. (2010). *Why race and culture matter in schools: Closing the achievement gap in America's classrooms.* New York, NY: Teachers College Press.

Hoy, W. (2012). School characteristics that make a difference for the achievement of all students: A 40-year odyssey. *Journal of Educational Administration,* 50(1), 76–97.

Hulpia, H., Devos, G., & Rosseel, Y. (2009). The relationship between the perception of distributed leadership in secondary schools and teachers' and teacher leaders' job satisfaction and organizational commitment. *School Effectiveness and School Improvement,* 20(3), 291–317.

Ingle, K., Rutledge, S., & Bishop, J. (2011). Context matters: Principals' sensemaking of teacher hiring and on-the-job performance. *Journal of Educational Administration,* 49(5), 579–610.

Kirby, M. M., & DiPaola, M. F. (2011). Academic optimism and community engagement in urban schools. *Journal of Educational Administration,* 49(5), 542–562.

Knapp, M. S., Honig, M. I., Plecki, M. L., Portin, B. S., & Copland, M. A. (2014). *Learning-focused leadership in action: Improving instruction in schools and districts.* New York, NY: Routledge.

Kurland, H., Peretz, H., & Hertz-Lazarowitz, R. (2010). Leadership style and organizational learning: The mediate effect of school vision. *Journal of Educational Administration, 48*(1), 7–30.

Lee, V. E., & Smith, J. B. (1999). Social support and achievement for young adolescents in Chicago: The role of school academic press. *American Educational Research Journal, 36*(4), 907–945.

Leithwood, K., & Louis, K. S. (2012). *Linking leadership to student learning.* San Francisco, CA: Jossey-Bass.

Leithwood, K., & Mascall, B (2008). Collective leadership effects on student achievement. *Educational Administration Quarterly 44*(4), 529–561.

Leithwood,K., Patten, S., & Jantzi, D. (2010). Testing a conception of how school leadership influences student learning. *Educational Administration Quarterly, 46*(5), 671–706.

Licata, J. W., & Harper, G. W. (2001). Organizational health and robust school vision. *Educational Administration Quarterly, 37*(1), 5–26.

Marks, H. M., & Printy, S. M. (2003). Principal leadership and school performance: An integration of transformational and instructional leadership. *Educational Administration Quarterly, 39*(3), 370–397.

Marshall, C., Patterson, J. A., Rogers, D. W., & Steele, J. R. (1996). Caring as career: An alternative perspective for educational administration. Educational Administration Quarterly, 32(2), 271–294

Martin, Emmie. (2015). "4 ways to outsmart any multiple-choice test," Business Insider, Retrieved from: http://www.businessinsider.com/4-ways-to-outsmart-any-multiple-choice-test-2015-6

May, H., & Supovitz, J. A. (2011). The scope of principal efforts to improve instruction. Educational Administration Quarterly, 47(2), 332–352

McLaughlin, M. W., & Talbert, J. E. (2001). *Professional communities and the work of high school teaching.* Chicago, IL: University of Chicago Press.

Mintrop, H. (2012). Bridging accountability obligations, professional values and (perceived) student needs with integrity. *Journal of Educational Administration, 50*(5), 695–726.

Mitchell, C., & Sackney, L. (2006). Building schools, building people: The school principal's role in leading a learning community. *Journal of School Leadership, 16*(5), 627–640.

Murphy, J. (2011). *Essential lessons for school leaders.* Thousand Oaks, CA: Corwin.

Murphy, J., & Torre, D. (2014). *Creating productive cultures in schools for students, teachers, and parents.* Thousand Oaks, CA: Corwin.

National Association of Elementary School Principals (2008). *Leading learning communities: Standards for what principals should know and be able to do.* Reston, VA: Author.

National Association of Secondary School Principal (2014). *Breaking ranks: 10 skills for successful school leaders.* Reston, VA: Author.

Nelson, S. W., & Guerra, P. L. (2013). Educator beliefs and cultural knowledge implications for school improvement efforts. *Educational Administration Quarterly, 50*(1), 67–95.

Opfer, V. D. (2006). Evaluation equity: A framework for understanding action and inaction on social justice issues. *Educational Policy, 20*(1), 271–290.

Orr, M. T., Berg, B., Shore, R., & Meier, E. (2008). Putting the pieces together: Leadership for change in low-performing schools. *Education and Urban Society, 40*(6), 670–693.

Penuel, W. R., Riel, M., Joshi, A., Perlman, L., Kim, C. M., & Frank, K. A. (2010). The alignment of the informal and formal organizational supports for reform: Implications for improving teaching in schools. *Educational Administration Quarterly, 46*(1), 57–95.

Printy, S. M. (2008). Leadership for teacher learning: A community of practice perspective. *Educational Administration Quarterly, 44*(2), 187–226.

Reitzug, U. C., & Patterson, J. (1998). I'm not going to lose you! Empowerment through caring in an urban principal's practice with students. *Urban Education, 33*(2), 150–181.

Riehl, C. L. (2008). The principal's role in creating inclusive schools for diverse students: A review of normative, empirical, and critical literature on the practice of educational administration. *Journal of Education, 189*(1/2), 183–197.

Robinson, V., Lloyd, C., & Rowe, K. (2008). The impact of leadership on student outcomes: An analysis of the differential effects of leadership types. *Educational Administration Quarterly, 44*(5), 635–674.

Rodriguez, L. (2008). Teachers know you can do more: Understanding how school cultures of success affect urban high school students. *Educational Policy, 22*(5), 758–780.

Sebastian, J., & Allensworth, E. (2012). The influence of principal leadership on classroom instruction and student learning: A study of mediated pathways to learning. *Educational Administration Quarterly, 48*(4), 626–663.

Shapiro, J. P., & Stefkovich, J. A. (2010). *Ethical leadership and decision making in education: Applying theoretical perspectives to complex dilemmas* (3rd ed.). New York, NY: Routledge.

Skrla, L., Scheurich, J. J., Barcia, J., & Nolly, G. (2004). Equity audits: A practical leadership tool for developing equitable and excellent schools. *Educational Administration Quarterly, 40*(1), 133–161.

Smylie, M. A. (2010). *Continuous school improvement.* Thousand Oaks, CA: Corwin.

Spillane, J. P., Halverson, R., & Diamond, J. S. (2001). Investigating school leadership practice: A distributed perspective. *Educational Researcher, 30*(3), 23–28.

Stoll, L., Bolam, R., McMahon, A., Wallace, M., & Thomas, S. (2006). Professional learning communities: A review of the literature. *Journal of Educational Change, 7*(4), 221–258.

Supovitz, J. (2002). Developing communities of instructional practice. *Teachers College Record, 104*(8), 1591–1626.

Supovitz, J., Sirinides, P., & May, H. (2010). How principals and peers influence teaching and learning. *Educational Administration Quarterly, 46*(1), 31–56.

Terosky, A. L. (2013). From a managerial imperative to a learning imperative: Experiences of urban, public school principals. *Educational Administration Quarterly, 50*(1), 3–33.

Thapa, A., Cohen, J., Guffey, S., & Higgins-D'Alessandro, A. (2013). A review of school climate research. *Review of Educational Research, 83*(3), 357–385.

Theoharis, G. (2009). *The school leaders our children deserve: Seven keys to equity, social justice, and school reform.* New York, NY: Teachers College Press.

Thoonen, E. E., Sleegers, P. J., Oort, F. J., Peetsma, T. T., & Geijsel, F. P. (2011). How to improve teaching practices: The role of teacher motivation, organizational factors, and leadership practices. *Educational Administration Quarterly, 47*(3), 496–536.

Warren, M., Hong, S., Rubin, C., & Uy, P. (2009). Beyond the bake sale: A community-based relational approach to parent engagement in schools. *Teachers College Record, 111*(9), 2209–2254.

Wayman, J. C., & Stringfield, S. (2006). Data use for school improvement: School practices and research perspectives. *American Journal of Education, 112*(4), 463–468.

Ylimaki, R. M. (2006). Toward a new conceptualization of vision in the work of educational leaders: Cases of the visionary archetype. *Educational Administration Quarterly, 42*(4), 620–651.

Ylimaki, R. M. (2012). Curriculum leadership in a conservative era. *Educational Administration Quarterly, 48*(2), 304–346.

York-Barr, J., & Duke, K. (2004). What do we know about teacher leadership? Findings from two decades of scholarship. *Review of Educational Research, 74*(3), 255–316.

Youngs, P., & King, M. B. (2002). Principal leadership for professional development to build school capacity. *Educational Administration Quarterly, 38*(5), 643–670.

About the Author

Dr. Wafa Hozien has been preparing students to pass the SLLA exam since 2008, when the test was originally a six-hour paper-and-pencil test. She has come up with innovative strategies that are timely and have led to success for every student that she prepares for the exam. Her professional background includes over 20 years' work as a special and regular education teacher, a high school history teacher, and a school administrator.

Dr. Hozien has designed and delivered training for leadership academies throughout the United States and internationally. She specializes in combining research-based strategies and practical applications, working with teacher leaders, school administrators, and school districts to adapt innovative strategies for their locations.

Presently, she is Assistant Professor of Educational Leadership at Central Michigan University and teaches graduate courses in preparing aspiring school leaders to be at their best in any given school setting. Dr. Hozien appreciates constructive feedback and gaining insight as to best practices and ways to improve the SLLA preparation process. If you find that this book is missing something or suggestions for improvement, then kindly contact the author via e-mail; Dr. Hozien can be reached at whozien@gmail.com